Teach Terrific WRITING

PERFECT FOR · TEACHERS OF GRADES 4-5

Teach Terrific WRITING

Gary Robert Muschla

New York   Chicago   San Francisco   Lisbon   London   Madrid   Mexico City
Milan   New Delhi   San Juan   Seoul   Singapore   Sydney   Toronto

2 3 4 5 6 7 8 9 10 11 12 13 14 15 16 17 18 19 20 21   QPD/QPD   0 9 8

ISBN 978-0-07-146316-4
MHID   0-07-146316-X
Library of Congress Control Number: 2006924893

Interior design by Nick Panos

McGraw-Hill books are available at special quantity discounts to use as premiums and sales promotions or for use in corporate training programs. To contact a representative, please visit the Contact Us pages at www.mhprofessional.com.

This book is printed on acid-free paper.

Contents

Reproducible Worksheets

Personally Speaking

Among Friends

School Days

Near and Far

Leisure Time

Recreation

Weird, Strange, and Unbelievable

Part 2
Writing the Draft

Reproducible Worksheets

Part 3
Revision

Reproducible Worksheets

Part 4
Proofreading

Reproducible Worksheets

About This Book

Learning to write is a challenging, multiskilled process. Students must learn how to identify, analyze, and develop ideas. They must learn how to compose sentences, build paragraphs, and express ideas within the standards of written English. They must discover their "voice" and learn how to precisely say what they want with fluency, clarity, and energy.

Teach Terrific Writing, Grades 4–5 can be a valuable resource as you guide your students through this process. The teaching suggestions, exercises, and reproducible worksheets will enable you to provide your students with meaningful writing assignments and activities. Your students will learn how to find and focus ideas for writing, how to write a draft, how to revise their writing, and how to proofread their work. This book, which is based on the stages of the writing process, will give students the practice they need to acquire the skills for effective composition and to grow as young writers.

Helping your students learn to write is a difficult task. It is my hope that you will find this book useful in that demanding and rewarding challenge.

How to Use This Book

Teach *Terrific Writing, Grades 4–5* is divided into four parts that concentrate on writing skills, from developing ideas to proofreading, and provide teaching suggestions, exercises, and reproducible worksheets. The book includes an answer key.

Part 1 Finding and Developing Ideas for Writing, begins with the understanding that solid ideas are the backbone of good writing. Although ideas are all around, young writers need to learn how to identify and develop ideas for their writing. This section includes information on idea development, teaching suggestions, six exercises, and one hundred reproducible worksheets designed to help students develop material for writing. The worksheets are broken down into seven sections: "Personally Speaking," "Among Friends," "School Days," "Near and Far," "Leisure Time," "Recreation," and "Weird, Strange, and Unbelievable." Each worksheet offers students a topic and guidelines they can use to explore and develop the topic.

Part 2 Writing the Draft, focuses on skills that help students to write with competence and confidence. Along with teaching suggestions and information on the characteristics of good writing, eleven exercises and twenty reproducible worksheets address topics such as using proper sentence structure, combining and varying sentences, constructing paragraphs, using active constructions and strong verbs, and choosing a point of view.

Part 3 Revision, focuses on skills and methods necessary for effective revision. Teaching suggestions, two exercises, a reproducible Guidelines for Revision, and twenty-five reproducible worksheets are included. Worksheets, which include both fiction and nonfiction, show students the types of weak composition that can slip into their own writing. Students are required to identify and revise the weaknesses on the worksheets.

Part 4 Proofreading, examines the skills and methods necessary for effective proofreading. Teaching suggestions, three exercises, a reproducible Guidelines for Proofreading, and twenty-five reproducible worksheets are included in this section. The worksheets, both fiction and nonfiction, present students with the errors in mechanics they will undoubtedly find in their own writing. As students find and correct the errors on the worksheets, they will gain critical skills for proofreading their own work.

Answer Key includes solutions for the worksheets. In cases where answers vary (for example, revision), possible answers are provided.

The background material, teaching suggestions, exercises, and reproducible worksheets are designed to make your teaching easier. Each worksheet stands alone, can be used with students of varying abilities, and is set up in a clear, easy-to-follow format. The worksheets can serve as the basis of your writing program, you may use them to supplement the lessons of your language arts instruction, or you may use them as reviews for material previously taught or as extra-credit assignments. You can even use them with substitute plans. Use the worksheets in whichever manner is most beneficial to your students.

The reproducible worksheets and exercises offer more than 190 separate activities. They will provide your students with a rich variety of writing experiences and help them gain a better understanding of the writing process.

Finding and Developing Ideas for Writing

Good writing begins with a good idea. Without an interesting idea, even the most skillful writing will result in an unremarkable piece. At best, the reader will plod through such a piece, hoping to find something of value; at worst, he or she will quickly conclude there is nothing of value and put the piece aside.

Aware of the importance of ideas, professional authors spend significant effort and time identifying, developing, researching, analyzing, and organizing ideas before they begin writing. They understand that if they start writing with fuzzy, unclear ideas, they will write with little focus or direction. Instead of writing with purpose and efficiency, they will write with confusion and frustration.

This is why it is essential that young writers learn how to discover and develop ideas for writing. Fresh ideas are the raw materials that build the foundation of effective expression.

Discovering Ideas

Just about every student has an abundance of ideas that can be the foundation of solid writing. Few, however, know how to find these ideas. They may not recognize how ideas are interrelated and how an idea can be expanded and refined—and sometimes entirely transformed—into new ideas that can become interesting pieces.

To help your students discover ideas for writing, you need to make them realize that they have a reservoir of ideas within themselves. Through reflection, imagination, and diligence, students can find much to write about. The starting point is personal experience.

Personal Experience: The Source

The seed of every idea takes root in the rich soil of personal experience. From that seed, the idea grows, branches, and, with the right care and nourishment, blossoms and blooms. Not only our direct experiences, but our dreams, our musings, things we hear about or learn, everything that we experience can be the substance of which an idea can be built.

The following are some examples of personal experiences that can generate ideas.

- A nightmare can provide the preliminary idea for a scary story.
- Seeing a flyer about a lost dog can lead to a story about a missing puppy.
- Learning about the Amazon basin can inspire an essay about the importance of the rain forests.
- Hearing about a big storm can remind a person about a major storm he experienced and lead to a narrative about survival.
- A friend's moving away can be the motivation for written reflection about friendship.

Children have countless experiences that can serve as initial ideas for writing. They simply need to be shown how to tap into their wealth of experience.

Exercise 1.1 Tapping into Personal Experience

Explain to your students that their personal experiences—all the things they have ever done, seen, read, or heard about—can lead to ideas they can use for writing. They must learn how to identify these ideas within their memories.

Write one of the following topics on an overhead projector or the board:

- Things That Are Important to Me
- The People in My Life
- Interests and Hobbies
- Things I Like
- Things I Dislike

Ask your students to volunteer examples that can be included under the topic, and then write their suggestions beneath the topic. For example, under "Interests and Hobbies," students might suggest examples such as reading, skateboarding, soccer, camping, model building, music—obviously, the list can get quite extensive.

After writing several examples, discuss how each can lead to an idea for writing. Here are some possibilities:

- For reading—a review of a favorite book
- For skateboarding—a description of some of the techniques necessary for "extreme" skateboarding
- For camping—a narrative about a fun camping trip

The Value of Keeping a Journal

Having students regularly write in a journal is an excellent method to tap into personal experience. In a writing journal, students can express their thoughts and feelings on topics they find meaningful. In time, a journal can become a warehouse of writing ideas ranging from whimsical musings to the deepest emotions.

Because journals tend to be personal and reflective and are a forum in which students frequently explore ideas, I do not recommend that journals be corrected or graded. When journals are graded, students are less willing to experiment with ideas and different forms of writing and often write more of what they feel will result in a good grade. This undermines the purpose of the journal, which should be a place a writer can write without concern for convention or form. For some students, their greatest growth as young writers first emerges in their journals.

Although you will find that many students will want to share their journals with you and their friends, student journals should be private unless you explain in advance that you will periodically read them. If you read journals, feel free to write comments, offer suggestions, pose questions to stimulate thinking, or simply share your thoughts. Students will appreciate the feedback.

Writing journals need not be lavish to be purposeful. A composition book or spiral notebook is sufficient. Some students like to keep their journals on their computers and e-mail some of their writing to their teachers. In whichever form students keep their journal, suggest that they date all entries, because dates provide a time reference that will help students to follow their progress as writers. Also suggest that students review their journals periodically to find ideas for writing.

The Value of Reading

Reading is yet another way to tap into personal experience in search of ideas. Reading can present us with new ideas, add information to old ideas, and stimulate reflection on ideas. Reading expands our world and experience.

The benefits of reading for writing go far beyond expanding our world and experiences, however. Reading also introduces young writers to various forms of writing, idea development, and authors' techniques. It is no coincidence that virtually all writers are readers.

Reading should play a prominent role in your classroom in support of writing. You should encourage reading, provide time for it, and make a variety of reading materials available for your students. Reading with and to your students can demonstrate your pleasure in reading and be a powerful model to students.

Seeing Life Through the Eyes of a Writer

Most writers view the world with a sharp eye. They see, they contemplate, and they ask themselves, "What if . . ." To help your students see the world through the eyes of a writer, encourage them to be both observers and interpreters of life. Encourage them to be inquisitive, curious, and open to new ideas. Encourage them to step outside themselves and try to look at things from the perspectives of others.

Offer this example. Their school is likely to be a familiar place to your students. Suggest that they imagine how it would appear to a new student from another state. What would be the most striking feature about their school? Would the student feel lost? Out of place? Afraid or anxious? Why might a new student feel this way? Go one step farther. Ask them how their school would seem to a new student from another country who does not speak English. Considering situations and issues from another's point of view can enhance understanding and broaden perspective. It also can lead to new ideas.

Along with viewing things from different perspectives, tell your students to always look for details, using their senses of sight, hearing, touch, taste, and smell. Explain that by paying close attention to their surroundings they can sharpen their powers of observation.

Offer this example. Ask your students to imagine they are standing in their yard or a park. What do they see? Trees? What kinds of trees? Big? Small? Evergreen or deciduous? What about animals? Do they see any birds? What kinds? Maybe they see a gray squirrel scampering along a branch. What do they hear? The rustle of leaves? The songs of birds? The barking of a dog in the distance? What does

Exercise 1.2 What Are the Details?

Instruct your students to select a corner or a part of the classroom. While sitting in their seats, they are to list as many details as they can about this part of the room. Tell them to use as many of their senses as possible, though especially sight and hearing. After they are done, have students share some of the details they found. Emphasize that sharp, clear details make ideas come alive.

Seeing through the eyes of a writer broadens the world, enabling a person to become aware of not just the most prominent features of things but the smallest details as well. This is a valuable skill for students that extends well beyond writing and into all aspects of life.

the air smell like? Clean? Fresh? Full of the scent of flowers? If the day is windy, how does the wind feel against their face? Against their body? Is it so strong that it pushes them backward? Is the wind cold? Warm? Humid? What about touch? Maybe the ground is soggy beneath their feet because of the previous night's heavy rain. What about taste? Maybe they are chewing spearmint-flavored gum (sugarless, of course) that makes their mouth feel fresh. Encourage your students to experience the world through their senses. Awareness of details sharpens perspectives and adds to the images that make up ideas.

Focusing Ideas

Once general ideas have been explored, they must be focused. Focusing an idea narrows it down so that the writer can concentrate on a specific angle. This is essential for further development.

Exercise 1.3 Focusing Topics

Write one of the following general topics, or a similar topic of your choosing, on an overhead projector or the board:

- Hobbies
- Fun Things
- Pets

Explain to your students that these are broad topics that lack focus for writing. Start with one of the topics and ask your students to offer focused examples for it. Write their suggestions beneath the topic. You may find it beneficial to do a second, or perhaps third, topic for reinforcement.

Here is an example:

Fun things . . . snowboarding . . . snowboarding at a ski lodge . . . the best snowboarding day of my life.

Note how the topics become more focused.
Here is another example:

Pets . . . dogs and cats . . . dogs . . . beagles . . . my beagle . . . finding Sleuth.

Note how the general topics proceed to a specific one (which refers to the time Sleuth, the beagle, got lost).

Of course, these are simple examples, but they will give students the concept of how to focus ideas. It should also become apparent to them that a focused idea is easier to write about.

Consider the topic "Studying." This is broad and unfocused. Does the topic mean studying in general? Or studying for tests? Or studying a particular subject? The topic does not offer much direction. However, the topic "How to Study for Math Tests" is focused and serves as a clear guide for the writer to develop the piece.

A focused topic not only provides a writer with direction, but also enables a writer to channel her attention and remain on topic. Focused topics are more likely to result in unified pieces in which all the material of the piece relates to a whole.

Developing Ideas

It is seldom that ideas for writing burst into a writer's consciousness in complete form. In most cases, ideas are discovered and then must be explored, analyzed, and developed. Through the process of development, ideas may be expanded, refined, or even rejected, only to be resurrected again in new forms. Sometimes an initial idea gives rise to new ideas that become the focal point of writing. Although developing ideas is hard work, there are steps you can take to make the process easier for your students. These steps include establishing a classroom open to new ideas, posing questions to aid development, identifying relationships, brainstorming, and researching.

Perhaps most important, you must establish a classroom atmosphere in which an appreciation of ideas is fostered and supported. Your classroom should be a place where students are comfortable to share their ideas without fear of mockery or sarcasm. Criticism is necessary to the evaluation of ideas, and it should be positive and constructive. Feelings and opinions in the classroom should always be respected, and ethnicities must be accepted. Students should feel at ease in pursuing the development of ideas and confident that their ideas will not be ridiculed.

One of the best strategies for developing ideas is to consider the five *W*s and *How*: *Who? What? Where? When? Why? How?* Although each of these questions may not be applicable for every idea, they are useful for most.

Exercise 1.4 Developing Ideas Using the Five *W*s and *How*

Using an overhead projector or the board, write "Lost Puppy" as a basic idea for a story. Ask your students how they might build a story from this initial idea. Walk them through the developmental process by writing the following:

- *What?* A puppy got lost.
- *When?* When did he get lost?
- *Where?* Where was he last seen?
- *Who?* Who are the people (and puppy) in this story?

Another strategy for developing ideas is to look for relationships. Explain to your students that nothing exists in isolation. Relationships may not be apparent at first, but everything is connected in some way to something else.

Offer this example. A honeybee visits a flower and takes some of its nectar. The bee returns to the hive, where the nectar is used to make honey. However, while the bee is on the flower, pollen necessary for plants to reproduce clings to the bee's body. As the bee visits other flowers, some of the pollen rubs off, making the plant's reproduction possible. This relationship is vital to both honeybees and flowers. Mature flowers, however, are important not only for honeybees. They may serve as food for rabbits or deer, be a hiding place for small animals, or simply beautify the countryside or someone's garden. Encouraging your students to recognize relationships between both living and nonliving things is a skill that can serve them well in whatever they do.

To reinforce this concept, point out and discuss relationships in the various subjects in your class whenever you can. Relationships can be complex, but basic ones are easy for students to grasp—for example, cause and effect (torrential rains cause floods), interdependence (honeybees and flowers), and parts to wholes (our solar system is a part of the Milky Way galaxy, which is a part of the universe). Make highlighting the connections between things a priority in your classroom, and in time your students will learn to look for and recognize relationships.

Brainstorming is another strategy students can use to develop ideas for writing. A mental exercise in which a person writes down as many ideas as he can about a topic, brainstorming can be a powerful method in the development of ideas. Explain to your students that the purpose of brainstorming is to write as many related ideas about a topic as quickly as possible. They should not pause to analyze ideas during brainstorming, because that only slows the generation of ideas. Evaluation may be done later. Brainstorming is a fast and furious exercise, the sole purpose of which is to expand ideas.

Explain to your students that creating a *word web* can help them identify, expand, and develop ideas for writing. On an overhead projector or the board, write the topic "School Lunchroom" in the middle of the page. (If you prefer, you might ask students to suggest a topic. Using a topic students provide assures them that the topic is genuine and not one you picked simply because it works for the activity.)

Ask students to volunteer ideas related to the school lunchroom. They might suggest ideas such as the following: noisy, fun, mystery food, recess, seeing friends, talking with friends, not much time to eat, and so on. As they offer ideas, write them down. Use a line to connect ideas that stem from other ideas. Write quickly and do not pause to discuss ideas now. Remind students that the goal of brainstorming is to uncover as many related ideas as possible and thereby expand the original idea.

When you are done, review the ideas the class generated. Explain that some of the ideas on the word web will probably not be used in writing, but others will. Sometimes a web will lead to an entirely new idea that may then lead to a new web and more new ideas for writing.

Although I do not demand that students complete word webs for the development of their ideas, I suggest they do. Brainstormed word webs can help students flesh out and expand initial ideas in a nonthreatening manner that yields fresh possibilities for writing.

Researching is yet another way students can develop ideas for writing. Along with traditional print sources, the Internet and electronic databases provide writers with broad resources for finding information on countless topics. Before the development of the Internet, writers often had to conduct extensive research in order to find information on some topics. Even then, they might not be able to find what they needed. Today, writers often find too much information.

Although you should encourage your students to use the Internet for research when developing writing topics, you should also provide them with guidelines that can help them find what they need. Most important, students need to understand that anyone can post information on the World Wide Web. Not all of the information students will find will be valid or useful. To minimize the chances of finding invalid data, caution your students to conduct research on reputable sites, which include the sites of government agencies, major organizations, and universities. Fortunately, many of the best sites often are listed first when doing a search.

To facilitate searching on the Internet, instruct your students to use specific key terms. Most search engines have become so sophisticated that using key terms directs searchers to sites that they will find useful. Certainly for students in fourth and fifth grades, the terms they would use for looking up information in an encyclopedia or other reference book will yield accurate results with most Internet search engines. Having a focused topic will provide students with guidance to keep on track during research, and can help keep them from becoming mired in huge amounts of irrelevant information.

Organizing Ideas

In their enthusiasm (some teachers would call this "rush") to complete their writing, many students take their ideas and want to begin writing immediately. The result is almost always the same: the aspiring writers finish pieces that are disorganized and require so much revision that they do not know where to start. Consequently, they do not do much revision, become dissatisfied with their work, and soon become convinced that they are poor writers.

Providing your students with simple techniques for organization will help them to clarify and order ideas, which makes writing easier. Although in the upper grades some writing (especially research reports) might benefit from detailed outlines, younger students benefit more from using a basic structure of opening, body, and closing for their writing. Convincing students of the need for organization is not easy, but if you keep emphasizing the necessity for a practical plan for writing, your students will eventually learn and use the basics of organization.

Exercise 1.6 Basic Organization for Nonfiction

Using an overhead projector or the board, write this simple form for structure. Discuss the parts with your students.

- **Opening:** One or two paragraphs
- **Body:** One, two, three, or more paragraphs
- **Closing:** One paragraph

It may help to write this form on poster paper and leave it on display in the room. Encourage students to refer to the form regularly during writing.

Explain the three parts of basic structure. The opening should introduce the topic and the problem or situation the writing is about. The body, which may be one paragraph, several paragraphs, or several pages long, provides information, including examples and details. The closing includes a final point or a brief summary of the main ideas expressed in the body.

Illustrate this form using an article from your students' reading program, social studies book, or science text. It is best to use an article for this activity, as the structure for fiction may not be as clear, especially to young writers.

Ask students to identify the opening of the article; then the body, including the paragraphs that make it up; and finally, the closing. Note that most nonfiction follows this format. Urge students to look for this form in the articles they read.

Helping Students Who Have Trouble Finding Ideas

Despite possessing many experiences that can be the seeds for ideas for writing, some students, through lack of motivation, weak skills, or poor confidence, find it difficult to identify and develop sound ideas. These students require more guidance from you than others.

For students you perceive as lacking motivation, work with them to find ideas that they consider to be interesting. I remember a student who did not like to write, but he liked activities such as dirt-bike racing and helping his father repair cars. Suggesting that he write about these kinds of topics stimulated a desire to share his knowledge of these subjects with others. During that year I learned more about dirt bikes than I will ever need to know, but the student wrote consistently and his skills improved significantly.

For students who possess weak skills, you should offer guidance in finding and developing ideas. Once they have identified an idea for writing, go on to the five *W*s and *How*. Make sure they answer each question about their topic with specifics; then help them organize their ideas. Having ideas formulated before writing makes the process of writing smoother.

For students who have poor confidence, talk with them and try to draw them out. Perhaps they are afraid that people might criticize their writing, or they may be concerned that they have nothing important to say. Assure these students that their ideas are as important as anyone else's. Show interest in what they have to say. Offer genuine praise, for example, "You did a nice job in describing that park," or "I could almost feel the rain pounding down on me." Explain that they should strive to develop their ideas fully and express them clearly.

For most students, offering them latitude in developing ideas fosters a sense of ownership in their writing. While assigning a general topic for writing, encourage them to develop their ideas and express their thoughts as they wish. The worksheets at the end of this section provide students with assignments in which they have the freedom to develop their ideas in ways meaningful for them. This is an environment in which writing can thrive.

Reproducible Worksheets

The following reproducible worksheets can help you to develop your students' basic writing skills. The one hundred worksheets are divided into seven sections:

- Personally Speaking
- Among Friends
- School Days
- Near and Far
- Leisure Time
- Recreation
- Weird, Strange, and Unbelievable

The themes of the worksheets in each category are loosely based on the title of the category. For example, the worksheets contained in "Personally Speaking" focus on the author in some way. The worksheets in "Recreation" focus on sports or some type of recreation.

While most of the worksheets are to be developed as articles, narratives, or persuasive pieces, several fiction topics are included throughout the categories, with the most fiction appearing in the final category, "Weird, Strange, and Unbelievable." Select the worksheets that you feel will best serve the needs of your students.

Intended to be a prewriting activity, each worksheet is designed to help students conceive ideas for writing on a topic. Most of the topics tie into the experiences of students, making it easier for them to generate material for writing. Moreover, because the topics are general, students have much freedom to develop their ideas. For example, with Worksheet 1.4, "The Future Me," students are given the general idea of considering what they might be like in the future. They can pick a time a year from now, a few years from now, or many years from now. Answering the questions on the worksheet will stimulate the imaginations of students and present possibilities for writing. From that point, each student can develop the piece in his or her own way. For example, he or she may expand the material through brainstorming and word webbing. In some cases, to fully develop his or her ideas, a student may find it helpful to conduct research via print sources or the Internet.

When assigning any of the worksheets, make sure that your students understand what they are to write about. Also make sure they understand terms such as *article*, *narrative*, and *persuasive piece*, as well as terms for fiction, including *characters*, *setting*, *plot*, *action*, and *climax*.

Explain to your students that they are to complete the worksheet, using the back of the sheet or an extra sheet of paper if they need more space to answer the questions. Depending on your class, you may want to discuss the questions and offer some suggestions for development. After completing the worksheet, encourage your students to expand their ideas and add more details if necessary. Emphasize that the worksheets are guides. Students may find that not all the information they supply in response to the questions on the worksheets will wind up in their writing, and that sometimes information not related to the questions will. Suggest that they may choose a new title that more accurately reflects their writing. Realizing that ideas can be developed in a variety of ways is essential for idea development to flourish. Encourage your students to organize their ideas before writing and follow a basic plan of opening, body, and closing.

The purpose of any prewriting activity is to engage the writer's mind with the writing to be done. Once the process is begun, the only limits are the writer's imagination and enthusiasm.

1.1 An Autobiographical Sketch

Directions: An *autobiography* is a true story that a person writes about himself or herself. An *autobiographical sketch* is a short autobiography. Think about your life. Answer the questions and write an autobiographical sketch. Be sure to include an opening, body, and closing in your writing. Support your ideas with details and examples.

1. Briefly describe yourself (age, height, color of eyes, hair, and so on).

_____

_____

2. Name three things you like about yourself and why you like them.

_____

_____

_____

3. Name three things you dislike about yourself and why you dislike them.

_____

_____

_____

4. What would you most like to do this year? Why? _____

_____

_____

_____

1.2 My Family

Directions: Some families are big. Some are small. Every family is different from any other. Think about your family and what makes it special. Answer the questions and write an article about your family. Be sure to include an opening, body, and closing in your writing. Support your ideas with details and examples.

1. Who are the members of your family? _____

_____

_____

2. Briefly describe the members of your family. _____

_____

_____

_____

3. Describe some things that make your family special. _____

_____

_____

_____

4. What do you feel is the best thing about your family? Explain.

_____

_____

_____

_____

1.3 Pets and Me

Directions: Think about a pet. (If you do not have a pet, imagine that you can have any pet you wish.) Answer the questions below and write an article about your pet. Remember to include an opening, body, and closing in your writing. Support your ideas with details and examples.

1. What kind of pet do you have? _____

2. Describe how your pet looks. _____

_____

_____

3. Describe your pet's favorite place in your home. _____

_____

_____

4. Describe how your pet acts. _____

_____

_____

5. Describe what your pet likes to do most. _____

_____

_____

6. How do you help take care of your pet? _____

_____

14 The Future Me

Directions: Pick a time in the future. The time might be a year from now, a few years from now, or many years from now. Imagine yourself in that time. Answer the questions and write about yourself in the future. Be sure to include an opening, body, and closing in your writing. Support your ideas with details and examples.

1. What is the time of this story? _____

2. Where will you be living in the future? _____

3. Describe yourself in the future. _____

_____

4. What will you be doing? (For example, will you still be going to school? Will you have a job? What kind?) _____

_____

5. Describe your family and friends in the future. _____

_____

_____

6. What problems might you face in the future? _____

_____

7. What might you know in the future you do not know now?

_____

_____

1.5 Advice for Younger Students

Directions: Imagine that you can offer advice to students who will be in your class next year. Answer the questions and write an article about what they can expect. Be sure to use an opening, body, and closing in your writing. Support your ideas with details and examples.

1. What class are you in now? _____

2. What subjects do you study in this class? _____

_____

3. What materials will new students need to bring to class? _____

_____

_____

4. How can new students be successful in this class? _____

_____

_____

5. What would you like to warn new students about? _____

_____

_____

6. What is the best advice you can give them? _____

_____

_____

1.6 An Important Lesson

Directions: Think of a time you learned an important lesson. Answer the questions and write a narrative about this experience and what you learned. Remember to include an opening, body, and closing in your writing. Support your ideas with details and examples.

1. What is the subject you are writing about? _____

_____

2. When did this happen? _____

3. Where did this happen? _____

4. Who was with you? _____

5. Describe what happened. _____

_____

_____

_____

6. Why did this happen? _____

_____

_____

7. What lesson did you learn? _____

_____

_____

1.7 My Greatest Goal

Directions: Think of your goals. Which one do you want to reach the most? Answer the questions and write an article about your greatest goal. Be sure to include an opening, body, and closing in your writing. Support your ideas with details and examples.

1. What is your greatest goal? _____

_____

_____

_____

2. Why is this your goal? _____

_____

_____

_____

3. What must you do to reach this goal? _____

_____

_____

_____

4. Do you expect to one day reach this goal? Explain. _____

_____

_____

_____

1.8 My Favorite Holiday

Directions: Think about all the holidays you enjoy. Decide which one you like best. Answer the questions and write an article about your favorite holiday. Be sure to include an opening, body, and closing in your writing. Support your ideas with details and examples.

1. What are some holidays you enjoy? _____

_____

_____

2. Which one is your favorite? Why? _____

_____

_____

3. With whom do you celebrate this holiday? _____

_____

_____

4. Describe how you celebrate this holiday. _____

_____

_____

5. If you could make this holiday even better, what would you do?

_____

_____

_____

1.9 My Hero

Directions: Think about a person you consider to be a hero. This person might have lived long ago or might be living now. Answer the questions and write an article about your hero. Be sure to include an opening, body, and closing in your writing. Support your ideas with details and examples.

1. Describe three qualities a hero must have. _____

_____

_____

2. Who is a hero to you? _____

_____

3. Why do you feel this person is a hero? _____

_____

_____

_____

4. Is this person a hero to others? Explain. _____

_____

_____

_____

1.10 Highlights of the Day

Directions: Think about all the things you did yesterday. Did you finish all you wanted to do? Answer the questions and write a narrative about the day that just passed. Be sure to include an opening, body, and closing in your writing. Support your ideas with details and examples.

1. What did you do in the morning? _____

_____

_____

2. What did you do in the afternoon? _____

_____

_____

3. What did you do in the evening? _____

_____

_____

4. What was your most important accomplishment? Explain. _____

_____

_____

5. What did you not finish? Explain. _____

_____

_____

_____

1.11 My Greatest Responsibilities

Directions: Think of your responsibilities. Some of your responsibilities might include doing well in school, watching a younger brother or sister, or taking care of a pet. Answer the questions and write an article about your responsibilities. Be sure to include an opening, body, and closing in your writing. Support your ideas with details and examples.

1. What are some of your responsibilities? _____

_____

_____

2. What is your most important responsibility? _____

_____

_____

3. Give some examples of how you handle this responsibility. _____

_____

_____

4. Why is this responsibility the most important? _____

_____

_____

5. How do you feel about this responsibility? _____

_____

_____

1.12 An Exciting Event

Directions: Think of a time you took part in or watched an exciting event. Answer the questions and write a narrative about this experience. Be sure to include an opening, body, and closing in your writing. Support your ideas with details and examples.

1. What was the event? _____

2. When did the event take place? _____

3. Where did it take place? _____

4. Who was with you? _____

5. Describe what happened at the event. _____

_____

_____

_____

6. Why was the event exciting? _____

_____

_____

7. What was the best part of the event? _____

_____

_____

_____

1.13 Someone I Admire

Directions: Think about a person you admire. This person might be living, or he or she might have lived in the past. Answer the questions and write an article about this person. Be sure to include an opening, body, and closing in your writing. Support your ideas with details and examples.

1. Who is the person you admire? _____

2. How do you know this person? _____

3. Describe this person. _____

_____

_____

_____

4. What is special about this person? _____

_____

_____

_____

_____

5. Why do you admire this person? _____

_____

_____

_____

1.14 A Special Talent

Directions: Everyone has special talents. Think about what you do better than other people. Answer the questions and write about your special talent. Be sure to include an opening, body, and closing in your writing. Support your ideas with details and examples.

1. What is your special talent? _____

2. What skills or knowledge does this talent require? _____

_____

_____

3. How did you develop this talent? _____

_____

_____

_____

4. What advice could you give others so that they may develop this talent?

_____

_____

_____

5. How might you improve your special talent? _____

_____

_____

_____

1.15 One of the Most Important Things in My Life

Directions: Think about something or someone that is important to you. Answer the questions and write an article about what is important in your life. Be sure to use an opening, body, and closing in your writing. Support your ideas with details and examples.

1. What is most important to you? _____

_____

_____

2. Why is this important? _____

_____

_____

_____

_____

3. What do you do to show that this is important to you? _____

_____

_____

_____

4. How would your life be different if this was not a part of your life?

_____

_____

_____

1.16 What's a Friend?

Directions: Think about your friends. What makes a person a friend? Answer the questions and write an article explaining what you believe a friend is. Be sure to include an opening, body, and closing in your writing. Support your ideas with details and examples.

1. What is one trait of a friend? Give an example of this trait.

_____

_____

_____

2. What is a second trait of a friend? Give an example of this trait.

_____

_____

_____

3. What is a third trait of a friend? Give an example of this trait.

_____

_____

_____

4. What is the most important trait a friend should have? Explain.

_____

_____

_____

Among Friends

1.17 Rules for Getting Along with Others

Directions: Think about people you know who get along well with others. Now think about some people who do not get along with others. Answer the questions; then write an article about rules people should follow to get along with others. Be sure to include an opening, body, and closing in your writing. Support your ideas with details and examples.

1. Write one rule people should follow if they hope to get along with others. Why is this rule important?

_____

_____

_____

2. Write a second rule people should follow if they hope to get along with others. Why is this rule important?

_____

_____

_____

3. Write a third rule people should follow if they hope to get along with others. Why is this rule important?

_____

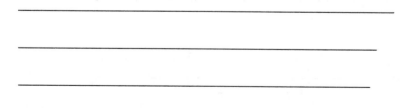

_____

_____

_____

1.18 Fun with Friends

Directions: Think of a great time you had with a friend. Maybe you went to a party, a sports event, or an amusement park. Or maybe you just hung out. Answer the questions; then write a narrative about a fun time you had with a friend. Be sure to include an opening, body, and closing in your writing. Support your ideas with details and examples.

1. Who is your friend? _____

2. Where did you go? _____

3. When did you go? _____

4. Who else was present? _____

   _____

5. How did you get there? _____

   _____

6. Describe this fun time. What did you do? _____

   _____

   _____

7. Why was this time so much fun? _____

   _____

   _____

   _____

Among Friends

1.19 A Friendly Adventure

Directions: Think about a time a friend and you shared an adventure. Answer the questions and write a narrative about your adventure. Be sure to include an opening, body, and closing in your writing. Support your ideas with details and examples.

1. Where did this adventure take place? _____

2. When did this adventure take place? _____

3. Who was with you? _____

4. Describe the scene of this adventure. _____

_____

_____

5. What happened? _____

_____

_____

_____

6. How did the adventure end? _____

_____

_____

_____

_____

1.20 A Friend in Need

Directions: Good friends are always willing to help each other. Think of a time you helped a friend. Answer the questions and write a narrative about this experience. Be sure to include an opening, body, and closing in your writing. Support your ideas with details and examples.

1. Who is your friend? _____

2. How long have you been friends? _____

3. When did you help your friend? _____

4. Why did he or she need help? _____

_____

_____

5. How did you help? _____

_____

_____

_____

6. What happened after you helped? _____

_____

_____

_____

_____

1.21 Friendly Letter

Directions: Think of a great novel or story you read. Now think of a friend who you believe would enjoy this book. Answer the questions; then write a letter to your friend to convince him or her to read this book. In your letter, try to show your friend why he or she would like this book, but do not reveal the book's ending.

1. What book would you like your friend to read? Who is the author?

_____

2. Describe the main characters in the book. _____

_____

_____

3. Describe the book's plot (but do not reveal the ending). _____

_____

_____

4. Why did you like this book? _____

_____

_____

5. Why do you think your friend would like this book? _____

_____

_____

_____

Among Friends

1.22 A Character Friend

Directions: Think of some favorite characters in some of your favorite stories or novels. Which of these characters would you most like to have as a friend? Answer the questions; then write an article explaining why this character would make a good friend. Be sure to include an opening, body, and closing in your writing. Support your ideas with details and examples.

1. What is the name of the character you would like to have as a friend?

_____

2. What is the title of the story where you first "met" this character?

_____

3. Describe the story. _____

_____

_____

4. Describe the character. _____

_____

_____

5. Explain what traits this character has that would make him or her a good friend.

_____

_____

_____

_____

1.23 A Biographical Sketch of a Friend

Among Friends

> **Directions:** A *biography* is a true story of a person's life. A *biographical sketch* is a short biography. Answer the questions on this worksheet; then write a biographical sketch of a friend. Be sure to include an opening, body, and closing in your biography. Support your ideas with details and examples.

1. What is the name of your friend? _____

2. How old is your friend? _____

3. What is your friend's birthday? _____

4. Where was your friend born? _____

5. Describe your friend's family. _____

    _____

6. Does your friend have any pets? If yes, describe them. _____

    _____

7. Describe your friend. (Include what he or she likes and dislikes.)

    _____

    _____

8. What are your friend's plans for the future?

    _____

    _____

1.24 Secrets

Directions: Imagine that a friend tells you a frightening secret. What would you do? Answer the questions and write a story about this secret and what happens. Be sure to include interesting characters, an exciting plot, and a climax to your story.

1. What is your friend's name? _____

2. Describe him or her. _____

   _____

3. Name and describe any other main characters in the story. _____

   _____

4. What terrible secret does your friend share with you? _____

   _____

5. What must you do? _____

   _____

6. What happens next? _____

   _____

   _____

7. How does the story end? _____

   _____

   _____

Among Friends

1.25 When Friends Disagree

> **Directions:** Imagine two friends who have a fight. What might happen? How might they feel? Answer the questions and write a story about two friends who have a fight. Be sure to include interesting characters, an exciting plot, and a climax to your story.

1. What are the names of the main characters in your story? _____

_____

2. Describe each of the main characters. _____

_____

3. Describe the setting of the story. _____

_____

4. When did the argument happen? _____

_____

5. What caused the fight? _____

_____

6. Describe the fight. _____

_____

7. What happened after the fight? _____

_____

Among Friends

1.26 My School

Directions: Schools around the country are a lot alike. But each is a little different, too. Think about your school. What is it like? Answer the questions and write an article describing your school. Be sure to use an opening, body, and closing in your writing. Support your ideas with details and examples.

1. What is the name of your school? _____

2. What grades attend your school? _____

3. About how many students attend your school? _____

4. In what town and state is your school? _____

5. Describe your school (classrooms, gym, cafeteria, auditorium, playground, and so on). _____

_____

_____

6. What subjects do you learn in school? _____

_____

_____

7. Describe a typical school day. _____

_____

_____

School Days

1.27 How to Improve My School

Directions: *Persuasive writing* is an article a person writes about a problem and how it might be solved. Think about the good things in your school. Now think about things that can be improved. Answer the questions and write a persuasive article about how your school can be improved. Be sure to include an opening, body, and closing in your writing. Support your ideas with details and examples.

1. Name something in your school that you feel should be improved.

   _____

2. Why should this be improved? Explain. _____

   _____

   _____

3. What could students do to help improve this? _____

   _____

   _____

4. What could teachers do to help improve this? _____

   _____

   _____

5. What could parents do to help improve this? _____

   _____

   _____

1.28 School Uniforms

Directions: Many schools have a dress code. Some schools even require that students wear uniforms. Think about your feelings about wearing a uniform to school. Answer the questions and write an article about your feelings. Be sure to include an opening, body, and closing in your writing. Support your ideas with details and examples.

1. Does your school require students to wear uniforms? If yes, describe the

   uniforms. _____

   _____

   _____

2. What are some advantages of wearing school uniforms? _____

   _____

   _____

   _____

3. Why might students dislike wearing uniforms to school? _____

   _____

   _____

   _____

4. What is your opinion about school uniforms? Explain. _____

   _____

   _____

   _____

School Days

1.29 Guidelines for Picking a Student of the Month

Directions: Imagine that you are in charge of giving an award for the student of the month in your school. This award may be for excellence in a certain subject or for all subjects. It might be given to someone who does something special for the school. Answer the questions and write an article explaining your guidelines for this award. Be sure to include an opening, body, and closing for your article. Support your ideas with details and examples.

1. What is the name of your award? _____

2. What is the award for? _____

   _____

   _____

   _____

3. What will a student have to do to earn this award? _____

   _____

   _____

   _____

4. What will the award be? _____

   _____

   _____

   _____

© Gary Robert Muschla

School Days

1.30 School Food

1. What kinds of food does your school serve for lunch? _____

_____

_____

2. What foods would you like your school to serve for the main part of lunch?

_____

_____

3. What foods would you like for dessert? _____

_____

4. What types of beverages would you like served with lunch? _____

_____

_____

5. If your school has snack machines that students can use, what types of snacks should be offered?

_____

_____

_____

Name _____   Date _____

1.31 Should Students Have Homework?

Directions: Few students like homework. But most receive homework at least a few times each week. Think about how much homework you receive. Answer the questions and write an article explaining your feelings about homework. Remember to include an opening, body, and closing in your writing. Support your ideas with details and examples.

1. Why is homework important? _____

_____

_____

2. When might homework not be important? _____

_____

3. How much homework do you feel should be given each night? Explain.

_____

_____

4. Do you feel homework should be given on the weekends? Holidays?

   Explain. _____

_____

_____

5. Would it help or hurt students if they never got any homework? Explain.

_____

_____

School Days

© Gary Robert Muschla

42

1.32 Favorite Subjects

Directions: Think of all the subjects you are studying in school this year. Which are your favorites? Answer the questions and write an article about your favorite subjects. Be sure to include an opening, body, and closing in your writing. Support your ideas with details and examples.

1. List all the subjects you are studying this year. _____

_____

_____

2. Which are your favorites? _____

_____

_____

_____

3. Why are these your favorites? _____

_____

_____

_____

4. Do you ever use what you learn in these subjects outside of school?
    Explain. _____

_____

_____

_____

School Days

1.33 Should Schools Have Honor Rolls?

Directions: The purpose of an honor roll is to recognize students who achieve good grades. But some schools do not have honor rolls. People in these schools believe honor rolls are not needed. Does your school have an honor roll? If yes, should it be continued? If no, should one be started? Answer the questions; then write an article sharing your feelings about an honor roll in your school. Remember to include an opening, body, and closing in your writing. Support your ideas with details and examples.

1. List reasons why students may feel a school should have an honor roll.

_____

_____

_____

_____

2. List reasons why students may feel a school should not have an honor roll.

_____

_____

_____

_____

3. Should your school have an honor roll? Explain. _____

_____

_____

_____

School Days

1.34 A Description of My Classroom

Directions: Look about your classroom. Notice how things are arranged. Answer the questions and write a description of your classroom. Remember to include an opening, body, and closing in your writing. Be sure to include good details.

1. Start at one corner and look around your classroom. List some of the

    objects you see. _____

    _____

    _____

    _____

2. Write details of these objects (for example, size, shape, and color).

    _____

    _____

    _____

    _____

3. Describe the furniture and how it is arranged. _____

    _____

    _____

    _____

4. Describe any tables and study stations.

    _____

    _____

    _____

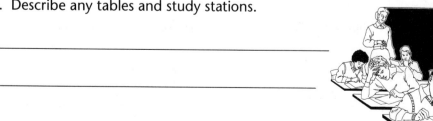

1.35 A Review of an Exciting Program

Directions: Your school probably has assemblies and other special events. For this writing assignment, take notes during an assembly or special event at your school. Answer the questions; then write a review. Be sure to include an opening, body, and closing in your writing. Support your ideas with details and examples.

1. What was the name of the program? _____

2. When and where was the program presented? _____

3. Who attended the program? _____

4. Who presented or starred in the program? _____

   _____

5. What was the program about? _____

   _____

6. Describe at least one thing you liked about the program. _____

   _____

7. Describe at least one thing you did not like about the program. _____

   _____

8. What was your opinion of the program? Explain. _____

   _____

   _____

1.36 The Best Things About My School

Directions: Most students like some things about their schools. For example, they might feel their school has the best kids, the best drama club, or the best band. Think about what you feel is best about your school. Answer the questions and write an article about your feelings. Be sure to include an opening, body, and closing in your writing. Support your ideas with details and examples.

1. What do you feel is best about your school? _____

_____

2. Provide reasons and examples why you feel this way.

Reason 1: _____

_____

Example: _____

_____

Reason 2: _____

_____

Example: _____

_____

Reason 3: _____

_____

Example: _____

_____

School Days

1.37 My Classroom Rules

Directions: Imagine that you could set up your classroom's rules. What rules would you make? Answer the questions and write about your classroom rules. Remember to include an opening, body, and closing in your writing. Support your ideas with details and examples.

1. Describe your classroom (include grade, number of students, size, and so on). _____

   _____

   _____

2. Write at least three rules you would make to help your classroom run smoothly. _____

   _____

   _____

   _____

3. How would these rules help your classroom run smoothly? _____

   _____

   _____

   _____

4. Do you think most students would agree that your rules are helpful? Explain. _____

   _____

   _____

School Days

1.38 A New Student

Directions: Imagine that your teacher has chosen you to show a new student around your school. Answer the questions and write a story about this. Include interesting characters, a plot, and a climax in your story.

1. Who is the new student in your story? _____

2. Describe him or her. _____

_____

_____

3. How might a new student feel in a new school? _____

_____

4. What places in your school would you show the new student? _____

_____

5. Why would you take the new student to these places? _____

_____

6. What (if anything) would you warn the new student about?

_____

7. Will the new student like your school? Explain. _____

_____

_____

School Days

1.39 My Perfect School

Directions: Imagine that you have the power to create a perfect school. This school could be everything you would want it to be. Answer the questions and write an article about your perfect school. Be sure to include an opening, body, and closing in your writing. Support your ideas with details and examples.

1. Where would your school be located? _____

2. How long would your school day be? _____

3. How long would your school year be? _____

4. What grades would your school have? _____

5. About how many students would be in each class? _____

6. What subjects would students in your school learn? _____

_____

7. What special features would your school have? (For example, a big gymnasium, a swimming pool, a playground?) _____

_____

8. What would be the most important rule in your school? _____

_____

9. Would students receive a good education at your school? Explain.

_____

140 Home Sweet Home

Directions: Think about where you live and what makes your home different from anyone else's. Answer the questions and write a description of your home. Remember to include an opening, body, and closing in your writing. Support your ideas with details and examples.

1. Where do you live? _____

2. Describe your neighborhood or the area around your home. _____

_____

3. Describe the climate where you live. _____

_____

4. Describe your house or apartment. _____

_____

_____

5. What is special about your home? _____

_____

_____

6. Do you like living there? Why or why not? _____

_____

_____

_____

Near and Far

1.41 Around City and Town

Directions: Imagine visitors coming to your city or town. They have never been here before and they do not know their way around. Answer the questions; then write a travel article about your city or town that explains where the most important places are. Be sure to include an opening, body, and closing in your writing. Support your ideas with details and examples.

1. List three places in your city or town (or in the area nearby) that visitors might be interested in seeing. _____

   _____

   _____

2. Describe each of these places. _____

   _____

   _____

   _____

   _____

   _____

3. Why might newcomers enjoy visiting these places? _____

   _____

4. What do you think visitors would like best about your city or town? _____

   _____

   _____

Near and Far

1.42 Traditions

Directions: Most cities and towns have special traditions. They might have a Founder's Day, a Memorial Day parade, or a fireworks display on the Fourth of July. Think about some of the traditions in the city or town where you live. Answer the questions and write an article about one of these traditions. Be sure to include an opening, body, and closing in your writing. Support your ideas with details and examples.

1. What is a tradition of your city or town? _____

_____

2. How often is this tradition celebrated? _____

3. Where is this tradition celebrated? _____

4. When is it celebrated? _____

5. Who takes an active part in the celebration? _____

_____

6. Describe this tradition or celebration. _____

_____

_____

7. What is your favorite part of this tradition? Explain. _____

_____

_____

Near and Far

1.43 Improvements

Directions: Think about how your city or town could be improved. Maybe more parks could be opened. Maybe there could be more activities for kids. Or maybe a public swimming pool could be built. Answer the questions and write an article about how your city or town could be improved. Remember to include an opening, body, and closing in your writing. Support your ideas with details and examples.

1. What is the name of your city or town? _____

2. Where is it located? _____

3. About how big is it? _____

4. Describe your city or town. _____

_____

_____

5. Name one thing that can be improved. _____

_____

6. Why should this be improved? _____

_____

_____

7. How might it be improved? _____

_____

_____

1.44 The Best Food Around

Directions: Think about the best restaurant you have ever eaten at in your city or town. Answer the questions and write an article explaining why this place is the best place to eat. Remember to include an opening, body, and closing in your writing. Support your ideas with details and examples.

1. What is the name of the best restaurant in your city or town?

_____

2. Describe this place. _____

_____

_____

3. With whom do you usually go to this place? _____

4. What kinds of food are served there? _____

_____

_____

5. Describe the best meal you have ever had there. _____

_____

_____

6. Explain why this place is a popular place to eat.

_____

_____

1.45 An Interesting State

Directions: Every state has many interesting places to visit. Think of your state and an interesting place you visited. Answer the questions and write an article about this place. Remember to include an opening, body, and closing in your writing. Support your ideas with details and examples.

1. What is the subject of this article? _____

2. Where is this place located? _____

3. When did you visit this place? _____

4. With whom did you go? _____

5. Describe this place. _____

_____

_____

6. Why is it interesting? _____

_____

_____

_____

7. Would you like to visit this place again? Explain. _____

_____

_____

1.46 My Place

Directions: Imagine being able to live anywhere you wanted. Answer the questions and write an article about this place. Be sure to include an opening, body, and closing in your writing. Support your ideas with details and examples.

1. Where would you like to live? _____

2. Describe this place. _____

   _____

   _____

   _____

3. Why would you like to live there? _____

   _____

   _____

4. What might be some disadvantages of living in this place? _____

   _____

   _____

5. Do you think you would ever get tired of living in this place? Explain.

   _____

   _____

   _____

Near and Far

1.47 The Best Vacation Ever!

Directions: Vacations can be times of great fun. Think of a vacation that you had. It might have been with your parents, relatives, or friends. Answer the questions and write a narrative about this vacation. Be sure to include an opening, body, and closing in your writing. Support your ideas with details and examples.

1. Where did you go for this vacation? _____

2. When did you go? _____

3. With whom did you go? _____

4. How did you get to your destination? _____

5. How long did you stay? _____

6. Describe the place you stayed at. _____

_____

_____

7. Describe what you did on your vacation. _____

_____

_____

8. What was the best part of your vacation? Explain.

_____

_____

Near and Far

1.48 A Travel First

Directions: Think back to a time when you first traveled in a train, sailed on a ship, flew in a plane, or maybe rode a horse. Answer the questions and write a narrative about this travel first. Be sure to include an opening, body, and closing in your writing. Support your ideas with details and examples.

1. What is the subject of your narrative? _____

2. How old were you when you first traveled in this way? _____

3. Where did you go? _____

4. Who was with you? _____

5. Describe your feelings about this travel first. _____

_____

_____

6. Did anything unusual happen on the trip? Explain. _____

_____

_____

7. Have you ever traveled like this again? If yes, explain how the other times were different from the first. _____

_____

_____

_____

Near and Far

1.49 Travel Advice

Directions: Imagine that a friend plans to go on vacation to a place that you have already visited. This might be a big amusement park, a cottage at a lake, or a large city. He or she asks you about this place and what to expect. Answer the questions; then write a letter of travel advice to your friend. Support your ideas with details and examples.

1. Where is your friend going on vacation? _____

2. What attractions might your friend expect to find there? _____

_____

3. Where would you suggest that he or she stay? Why? _____

_____

4. What kind of weather should your friend expect? _____

_____

5. What kinds of clothing should your friend bring? _____

_____

6. What types of equipment should your friend bring (for example, swimsuits, fishing poles, skis, sunglasses)? _____

_____

7. What would you warn your friend about? _____

_____

_____

Near and Far

1.50 Travel Calamity

Directions: Have you ever been traveling and had something go wrong? Maybe the car broke down. Maybe bad weather made your family miss their flight. Or maybe you went sailing and rough seas made you seasick. Imagine traveling and having everything go wrong. Answer the questions and write a story about a travel calamity. Create interesting characters, an exciting plot, and a climax for your story.

1. Name and describe the main characters in your story. _____

_____

_____

2. Where are the characters going? _____

3. Why are they going there? _____

_____

4. How are they traveling there? _____

5. Describe at least one thing that goes wrong. _____

_____

6. How do they solve their problem? _____

_____

7. Do they reach their destination on time? Explain. _____

_____

Near and Far

1.51 Vacation Mystery

Directions: A *mystery* is a story in which the characters try to solve a crime or figure out a puzzling problem. Mysteries can be as much fun to write as they are to read. Imagine going on vacation only to become involved in a mystery. Answer the questions and write a story about the mystery you must solve. Be sure to create interesting characters, an exciting plot, and a climax for your story.

1. Where and when does this story take place? _____

2. Name and describe the main characters in your story (be sure to include yourself). _____

_____

_____

_____

3. What is the mystery? _____

_____

_____

4. Name some clues that will help you solve the mystery. _____

_____

_____

5. How do you solve the mystery? _____

_____

_____

Near and Far

1.52 The Lost Puppy

Directions: Imagine that you or a friend has a puppy that gets lost. Answer the questions and write a story about how the puppy is found safe. Be sure to create interesting characters, an exciting plot, and a climax for your story.

1. Where and when does this story take place? _____

2. Name and describe the main characters. _____

_____

_____

3. Name and describe the puppy. _____

_____

_____

4. How does the puppy become lost? _____

_____

_____

5. How do the characters try to find the puppy? _____

_____

_____

6. How do they finally find the puppy? _____

_____

Near and Far

1.53 Stranger in Town

Directions: Imagine that a mysterious stranger comes to your town or neighborhood. This person has a secret. Answer the questions and write a story about this stranger. Be sure to create interesting characters, an exciting plot, and a climax for your story.

1. Where and when does the story take place? _____

2. Name and describe the main characters. _____

_____

_____

_____

3. What is unusual or mysterious about the stranger? _____

_____

_____

4. What secret does the stranger have? _____

_____

5. How do the other characters find out about the secret? _____

_____

6. How does the story end? _____

_____

_____

© Gary Robert Muschla

1.54 My Music

Directions: Think of your favorite kind of music. Answer the questions. Then write an article about the music you enjoy the most. Remember to include an opening, body, and closing in your writing. Support your ideas with details and examples.

1. What kind of music do you most like to listen to? _____

_____

2. Describe this type of music. _____

_____

3. What makes this type of music different from other kinds of music?

_____

4. Name some singers or groups who perform this type of music.

_____

5. Which is your favorite? Why? _____

_____

_____

6. Why do you like this type of music? Explain. _____

_____

_____

_____

Leisure Time

1.55 My Favorite Singer

Directions: Think about popular singers and musical groups. Who or which is your favorite? Answer the questions and write an article about this singer or group. Be sure to include an opening, body, and closing in your writing. Support your ideas with details and examples.

1. Who is your favorite singer or musical group? _____

2. What type of music does this singer or group perform? _____

3. What do you feel is the best song of this singer or group? Why do you feel

    this is the best? _____

    _____

    _____

4. How is this singer or group different from others? _____

    _____

    _____

    _____

5. Why is this singer or group your favorite? Explain. _____

    _____

    _____

    _____

    _____

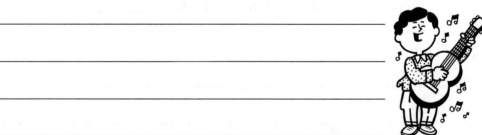

1.56 What the Song Says to Me

Directions: Most songwriters try to share ideas through their songs. The message they wish to share with their listeners is in the *lyrics* (or words) of the song. Choose a favorite song and think about the message of the songwriter. Answer the questions and write an article about what the song means to you. Be sure to include an opening, body, and closing in your writing. Support your ideas with details and examples.

1. What is the title of the song? _____

2. Who wrote and recorded the song? _____

3. What is the song about? _____

    _____

    _____

    _____

4. Which lyrics do you like the best? Why? _____

    _____

    _____

    _____

5. What is the message the songwriter is trying to share? Explain.

    _____

    _____

    _____

Leisure Time

1.57 A Book Review

Directions: A *book review* tells a reader what a book is about. It should include the reviewer's opinion of the book. Think about a book you recently read. Answer the questions and write a review of this book. Be sure to include an opening, body, and closing in your writing. Support your ideas with details and examples.

1. What is the title of your book? _____

2. Who is the author? _____

3. Who is the publisher? _____

4. When was the book published? _____

5. Is this book fiction or nonfiction? _____

6. Explain what the book is about. (For fiction, tell about the setting, characters, and plot, but do not tell the ending.) _____

_____

_____

_____

_____

7. Did you like this book? Explain. _____

_____

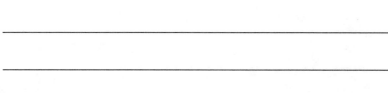

_____

_____

Leisure Time

1.58 Video Game Review

Directions: Writing a review of a video game can be a lot of fun. You have to play the game before you can write about it. Think of a video game you enjoy. Answer the questions and write a review of it. Remember to include an opening, body, and closing in your writing. Support your ideas with details and examples.

1. What is the name of the video game? _____

2. What age levels is it recommended for? _____

3. What must a player do to win? _____

_____

4. Describe the action of the game. _____

_____

_____

_____

5. What strategies can you suggest that will help a player to win?

_____

_____

6. Do you like this game? Why or why not? _____

_____

_____

Leisure Time

1.59 A Favorite Thing to Do

Directions: Think of something you enjoy doing—for example, sports, reading, or a hobby. Answer the questions and write an article about your favorite thing to do. Be sure to include an opening, body, and closing in your writing. Support your ideas with details and examples.

1. What is your favorite thing to do? _____

2. When and where do you enjoy this? _____

    _____

    _____

3. Describe your favorite thing to do. _____

    _____

    _____

    _____

    _____

    _____

4. Why is this your favorite thing to do? Explain. _____

    _____

    _____

    _____

Leisure Time

1.60 A Most Special Day

Directions: Imagine you could spend a day doing anything you wished. What would you do? Answer the questions and write an article about this special day. Remember to include an opening, body, and closing in your writing. Support your ideas with details and examples.

1. Where would you go on this special day? _____

2. Why would you go there? _____

_____

_____

3. With whom would you spend this day? _____

_____

4. Why would you choose this person or these people? _____

_____

_____

_____

5. Describe all you would do on this special day. _____

_____

_____

_____

_____

_____

Leisure Time

1.61 The Scariest Movie Ever!

Directions: Think of the scariest, most frightening movie you ever watched. Answer the questions and write an article about this movie. Be sure to include an opening, body, and closing in your writing. Support your ideas with details and examples.

1. What is the name of the movie? _____

2. What is the setting of the movie? _____

3. Who are the main characters? _____

    _____

4. What is the movie about? _____

    _____

    _____

5. Describe the scariest scene. _____

    _____

    _____

6. Why do you think this scene is so scary? Explain. _____

    _____

    _____

7. Would you recommend this movie to your friends? Explain. _____

    _____

1.62 TV in My Life

Directions: Think about how much TV you watch each day. Answer the questions; then write an article about TV in your life. Remember to include an opening, body, and closing in your writing. Support your ideas with details and examples.

1. About how much TV do you watch each day? _____

2. Do you think the amount of TV you watch is too much, just about right, or too little? Explain. _____

   _____

3. What types of TV shows do you enjoy the most? Why? _____

   _____

   _____

4. What types of TV shows do you enjoy the least? Why? _____

   _____

   _____

5. What is good about TV? Explain. _____

   _____

   _____

6. What is not good about TV? Explain. _____

   _____

   _____

Leisure Time

1.63 Character Changes

Directions: In most stories, the main characters change during the story. They may learn something new about themselves or about life. Think of one of your favorite characters in a story you read. Answer the questions and write an article about how the character changed. Be sure to include an opening, body, and closing in your writing. Support your ideas with details and examples.

1. What is the title of the story? _____

2. What is the name of the character? _____

3. Describe the story. _____

_____

4. Describe the character at the beginning of the story. _____

_____

_____

5. Describe the character at the end of the story. _____

_____

_____

6. Describe the changes in the character. _____

_____

7. What caused these changes? Explain. _____

_____

Leisure Time

1.64 A Fantasy Lunch

Directions: Imagine having lunch with a famous person of your choice. Answer the questions and write about your fantasy lunch. Be sure to include an opening, body, and closing in your writing. Support your ideas with details and examples.

1. With whom would you have lunch? _____

2. Why would you choose this person? _____

   _____

3. Where would you have lunch? _____

4. What would you have for lunch? _____

   _____

   _____

5. If you could ask this person three questions, what would they be?

   _____

   _____

   _____

6. What do you think the answers would be? _____

   _____

   _____

   _____

Leisure Time

1.65 A Great Product

> **Directions:** Think of a product you are very pleased with—for example, a pair of in-line skates, a new bike, or a DVD player for your room. Answer the questions and write an article describing this product to others. Remember to include an opening, body, and closing in your writing. Support your ideas with details and examples.

1. What is the product? _____

2. Where can people buy this product? _____

3. Describe what the product does. _____

   _____

   _____

   _____

   _____

4. Why are you so pleased with this product? _____

   _____

   _____

   _____

5. What, if anything, could make this product even better? Explain.

   _____

   _____

   _____

1.66 Changing Places

Directions: Imagine that you and a lead character of one of your favorite stories changed places. You are now the character in the story, and you change the ending. Answer the questions and write a new ending to the story. Create interesting characters, exciting action, and a climax for the new ending of the story.

1. What is the title of the story you are in? _____

2. Which character did you replace? _____

3. Name and describe the main characters in the story. _____

_____

_____

_____

4. Summarize the original story. _____

_____

_____

_____

_____

5. Describe the new ending. _____

_____

_____

_____

Leisure Time

1.67 The Un-Fun Funhouse

Directions: Imagine going in a funhouse that had no way out. Answer the questions and write a story about how you escaped this frightening funhouse. Create interesting characters, an exciting plot, and a climax for your story.

1. Where is the funhouse located? _____

2. Name and describe the main characters in your story. _____

_____

_____

3. Describe the funhouse. _____

_____

_____

_____

4. Why were you unable to find your way out? _____

_____

_____

_____

5. How did you finally escape the funhouse? _____

_____

_____

_____

Leisure Time

1.68 The Game

Directions: Think of a game you like to play. It might be a board game, a playground game, or a card game. Answer the questions and write an article about this game. Be sure to include an opening, body, and closing in your writing. Support your ideas with details and examples.

1. What is the name of this game? _____

2. When did you learn to play this game? _____

3. Who taught you how to play? _____

4. How many people can play the game at the same time? _____

5. Does the game require teams? Explain. _____

   _____

6. Describe the game (include its basic rules and how you win).

   _____

   _____

7. What strategies might someone use to win? _____

   _____

8. Why do you enjoy this game? Explain. _____

   _____

   _____

Recreation

1.69 My Favorite Sport

Directions: Think about the sports you enjoy playing or watching.
Answer the questions and write an article about your favorite sport.
Remember to include an opening, body, and closing in your writing.
Support your ideas with details and examples.

1. What is your favorite sport? _____

2. Explain which you enjoy doing more: playing or watching this sport.

_____

3. If teams are necessary, how many players are on a team? _____

4. Explain what, if any, special positions the team has. _____

_____

5. Where is this sport played? _____

6. What equipment do you need for this sport? _____

_____

7. Describe how a game is played in this sport. _____

_____

_____

8. Why do you like this sport? _____

_____

_____

1.70 Superstars

Directions: Think of an athlete you admire. This athlete might play a major sport like baseball or football, or an extreme sport like skateboarding or snowboarding. Answer the questions and write an article about this superstar and his or her sport. Be sure to include an opening, body, and closing in your writing. Support your ideas with details and examples.

1. Who is the superstar athlete? _____

2. In which sport is he or she a superstar? _____

3. Does this athlete play on a team? If yes, which one? _____

4. What position does he or she play? _____

5. How is this athlete more skilled than others who play this sport?

_____

6. What, if any, championships has this athlete won? _____

_____

7. What, if any, records has he or she broken? _____

_____

8. What makes this athlete a superstar? _____

_____

_____

1.71 A Perfect Day

Directions: Imagine that you could have a perfect day. You could go wherever you wanted and do whatever you wanted. Answer the questions and write about this perfect day. Remember to include an opening, body, and closing in your writing. Support your ideas with details and examples.

Morning

1. Where would you go? _____

2. Who would be with you? _____

3. What would you do? _____

Afternoon

1. Where would you go? _____

2. Who would be with you? _____

3. What would you do? _____

Evening

1. Where would you go? _____

2. Who would be with you? _____

3. What would you do? _____

What would be the most special part of the day? Why? _____

_____

1.72 Playground Safety

Directions: Imagine that you could write safety rules for your school's or neighborhood's playground. Answer the questions and write an article explaining your playground rules. Be sure to include an opening, body, and closing in your writing. Support your ideas with details and examples.

1. Do playgrounds need safety rules? Explain. _____

_____

2. What is the first rule you would want for a playground? Why is this rule

   important? _____

_____

_____

3. What is a second rule? Why is this rule important? _____

_____

_____

4. What is a third rule? Why is this rule important? _____

_____

_____

5. What might happen if people do not follow rules when using the

   equipment on a playground? Explain. _____

_____

_____

1.73 The Best

Recreation

Directions: Think of a time you were at your best. Maybe you were playing a game, such as soccer. Maybe you were playing in the school band at a concert. Maybe you were fishing with your grandfather and caught the biggest fish. Whatever you were doing, you were at your very best. Answer the questions and write a narrative about this day. Remember to include an opening, body, and closing in your writing. Support your ideas with details and examples.

1. What were you doing when you were at your best? _____

_____

_____

2. When and where were you at your best? _____

3. Who was with you? _____

4. Describe what made this day your best at what you were doing.

_____

_____

5. Describe how you felt being your best. _____

_____

_____

6. Did others realize you were at your best? Explain. _____

_____

1.74 Talent or Desire

Directions: Think about playing sports, playing a musical instrument, dancing, or being a cheerleader. What is more important to being successful, talent or desire? Answer the questions and write an article about which is more important. Be sure to include an opening, body, and closing in your writing. Support your ideas with details and examples.

1. What must a person do to become successful at sports, music, or other

   activities? _____

   _____

   _____

2. How important is talent to being successful? Explain. _____

   _____

   _____

3. How important is desire to being successful? Explain. _____

   _____

   _____

   _____

4. What, if any, other things might be important? Explain. _____

   _____

   _____

   _____

   _____

1.75 A Thrilling Time

> **Directions:** Think of a time you were at a thrilling event. For example, this might have been a championship football game, a cheerleading competition, or a monster truck show. Answer the questions and write about this time. Remember to include an opening, body, and closing in your writing. Support your ideas with details and examples.

1. What was this time? _____

2. Where and when did it take place? _____

3. Who was with you? _____

4. Describe the time. _____

   _____

   _____

   _____

5. What was the most thrilling part of the time? Why? _____

   _____

   _____

   _____

6. What was the least thrilling part of the time? Why? _____

   _____

   _____

   _____

1.76 A New Game

Directions: Have you ever invented a game or created new rules for an old game? Answer the questions; then write an article about a new game, or a new version of an old game, you invented. Remember to include an opening, body, and closing in your writing. Support your ideas with details and examples.

1. What is the name of your new game? _____

2. When did you invent this game? _____

3. Who, if anyone, helped you invent the game? _____

4. Describe the game and its rules. _____

_____

_____

_____

_____

5. How does a player win? _____

_____

_____

6. Have you played this game with others? If yes, did they like the game? Explain. _____

_____

_____

1.77 Being a Good Sport

Directions: Think about what it means to be a good sport. Answer the questions and write an article about being a good sport. Be sure to include an opening, body, and closing in your writing. Support your ideas with details and examples.

1. What does being a "good sport" mean? _____

_____

_____

_____

2. Give at least three examples of being a good sport. _____

_____

_____

_____

3. Is being a good sport important? Explain. _____

_____

_____

_____

4. Which is more important—winning or being a good sport? Explain.

_____

_____

_____

1.78 Report on a Sports Product

Directions: Think of sports equipment, such as a baseball glove, ice skates, or sneakers. Answer the questions; then write an article about a sports product, telling about its strengths and weaknesses. Be sure to include an opening, body, and closing in your writing. Support your ideas with details and examples.

1. What product is the subject of your article? _____

2. How often do you use this product? _____

3. Describe this product. _____

   _____

   _____

4. What do you like about this product? _____

   _____

   _____

5. What do you dislike about it? _____

   _____

   _____

6. Would you recommend this product to others? Explain. _____

   _____

   _____

Recreation

1.79 Special Doings

Directions: Think of a special activity that you enjoy with family or friends. Maybe you ride roller coasters with your cousin. Maybe you swim with friends in your pool. Or maybe you go camping with your parents. Answer the questions and write a narrative about your special doings. Remember to include an opening, body, and closing in your writing. Support your ideas with details and examples.

1. What is your special activity? _____

2. Who does this activity with you? _____

3. Where and when do you enjoy this special activity? _____

_____

4. Describe this activity. _____

_____

_____

_____

_____

5. What makes this activity special? Explain. _____

_____

_____

_____

_____

1.80 Great Competition

Directions: Think of a time you were in a great competition. Maybe you were in a dance competition. Maybe you were playing a tough computer game. Maybe you were in a race on the playground. Answer the questions and write a narrative about this great competition. Be sure to include an opening, body, and closing in your writing. Support your ideas with details and examples.

1. What was the competition? _____

2. Whom were you competing against? _____

3. When and where was this competition? _____

_____

4. Describe the competition. _____

_____

_____

5. What strategies did you use to try to win? _____

_____

_____

6. How did you win? Or why did you lose? Explain. _____

_____

_____

_____

1.81 Hey, Coach

Recreation

Directions: Imagine that you are a coach. You might be a soccer coach, a cheerleading coach, or a dance instructor. What advice could you give to younger students? Answer the questions and write an article about the advice you would give. Be sure to include an opening, body, and closing in your writing. Support your ideas with details and examples.

1. What sport or activity are you coaching? _____

2. How much experience do you have with this activity? _____

_____

_____

3. What do you like about this activity? _____

_____

_____

4. What skills should students have if they want to do well in this activity?

_____

_____

5. What advice would you give to younger students who are just starting this activity? _____

_____

_____

_____

1.82 The Big Game

Directions: Imagine being a sports star and playing in the biggest game of your life. Answer the questions and write a story about this game. Create interesting characters, an exciting plot, and a climax for your story.

1. What is the game in this story? _____

2. Name and describe the main characters. _____

    _____

    _____

3. Where and when does this story take place? _____

    _____

4. How does the story begin? _____

    _____

5. List three important things that happen in the story. _____

    _____

    _____

    _____

6. Describe how the story ends. _____

    _____

    _____

© Gary Robert Muschla

Recreation

1.83 UFOs (Unidentified Flying Objects)

Directions: Many people claim they have seen UFOs and beings from other planets. Answer the questions; then write an article sharing your feelings about UFOs. Be sure to include an opening, body, and closing in your writing. Support your ideas with details and examples.

1. Have you ever seen a UFO? If yes, where and when? _____

_____

2. Describe the UFO you saw. _____

_____

3. If you have not seen a UFO, do you believe they exist? Explain.

_____

4. Do you believe that life exists on other planets? If yes, explain why.

_____

_____

5. Do you believe beings from other planets have visited Earth? Explain.

_____

_____

6. If you do not believe that UFOs exist or that intelligent beings may live on

other planets, explain why. _____

_____

_____

1.84 Unexplained!

Directions: Everybody has seen or heard about strange events that cannot be explained. Answer the questions; then write about an unexplained event you have seen or heard about. Remember to include an opening, body, and closing in your writing. Support your ideas with details and examples.

1. What was the event? _____

2. Where and when did it happen? _____

_____

_____

3. Who was with you? _____

4. Describe the event. _____

_____

_____

_____

5. How did you, or others, try to explain what happened? _____

_____

_____

6. Why did the event remain unexplained? _____

_____

_____

Weird, Strange, and Unbelievable

1.85 Nightmare!

Directions: Everybody has nightmares. Some nightmares can be so scary that we wake up in the night with our hearts pounding. Answer the questions and write about your scariest nightmare. Be sure to include an opening, body, and closing in your writing. Support your ideas with details and examples.

1. Who is in your nightmare? _____

_____

_____

2. Where are you in your nightmare? _____

3. Describe the setting of your nightmare. _____

_____

4. Describe what happens in your nightmare. _____

_____

_____

_____

_____

5. Do you wake up during your nightmare? If yes, how do you feel?

_____

6. Are you afraid to go back to sleep after waking up? Why? _____

_____

Weird, Strange, and Unbelievable

1.86 Do You Believe in Magic?

Directions: Imagine being given magic powers, but your powers will allow you to cast only one magic spell. Answer the questions and write a story about your magic power. Create interesting characters, an exciting plot, and a climax for your story.

1. Name and describe the characters in your story. _____

_____

2. Where and when does the story take place? _____

_____

3. How did you receive your magic powers? _____

_____

_____

4. What one act of magic do you perform? _____

_____

_____

5. Why do you perform this act? _____

_____

6. What happens after you perform your magic? _____

_____

_____

Weird, Strange, and Unbelievable

1.87 It's a Dog's Life

Directions: Imagine if your dog, or another animal who knows you, could read and write. Now imagine if your dog kept a diary. Answer the questions and write a diary entry as if the entry had been written by your dog. Be sure to include great details in your writing.

1. Describe what your dog sees throughout the day. _____

_____

2. Describe what your dog hears throughout the day. _____

_____

3. Describe what your dog does most of the day. _____

_____

4. Describe what the best part of your dog's day is. _____

_____

_____

5. Describe what the worst part of your dog's day is. _____

_____

_____

6. Describe what your dog would say about you in the diary. _____

_____

_____

1.88 Reporter in the Past

Directions: Imagine that you are a reporter living in the past. You are writing about an important event that happened. Answer the questions and write an article about this event. Be sure to include an opening, body, and closing in your writing. Support your ideas with details and examples.

1. What event are you writing about? _____

2. When did this event take place? _____

3. Where did it take place? _____

4. Who was involved in the event? _____

_____

5. Describe the event. _____

_____

_____

6. Why did the event happen? _____

_____

_____

7. What happened after the event? _____

_____

_____

Weird, Strange, and Unbelievable

1.89 Coming Disaster

Directions: Imagine that you wake up one day with a feeling that a disaster is about to happen—and only you can stop it! Answer the questions and write a story of how you try to prevent this disaster. Create interesting characters, an exciting plot, and a climax for your story.

1. Where and when does your story take place? _____

_____

2. Name and describe the main characters in your story. _____

_____

_____

3. Describe the disaster that is about to happen. _____

_____

_____

4. What will you do to stop the disaster? _____

_____

_____

_____

5. Are you successful? Why or why not? _____

_____

_____

_____

Weird, Strange, and Unbelievable

1.90 Extraterrestrials in My School

Directions: Imagine that extraterrestrials, beings from another planet, have come to Earth. They are friendly and wish to learn about us. Some extraterrestrial students are visiting your school. You have been asked to show them around. Answer the questions and write a story about the extraterrestrials in your school. Create interesting characters, an exciting plot, and a climax for your story.

1. Name and describe the extraterrestrials who come to your school.

    _____

2. Where did the extraterrestrials come from? _____

    _____

3. Name and describe the human characters in your story. _____

    _____

4. Why were you chosen to show the extraterrestrials around? _____

    _____

5. What did you show them? _____

    _____

    _____

6. What did they find most interesting about your school? _____

    _____

    _____

Weird, Strange, and Unbelievable

1.91 Video Game Hero

> **Directions:** Think of your favorite video game. Imagine you are the star character of the game. Answer the questions and write a story about being a hero in a video game. Create interesting characters, an exciting plot, and a climax for your story.

1. What is the name of the video game? _____

2. Describe the setting of the game. _____

   _____

3. Name and describe the main characters in the game. _____

   _____

4. Describe the purpose of the game. _____

   _____

5. Describe your attempts to win the game. _____

   _____

6. How do your opponents try to stop you? _____

   _____

   _____

7. Do you win the game? Explain. _____

   _____

   _____

1.92 Oh, No! Enchanted!

Directions: Imagine that an evil witch casts a spell on you. This spell forces you to say whatever you are thinking. Answer the questions and write a story about this terrible spell. Create interesting characters, an exciting plot, and a climax for your story.

1. Name and describe the main characters in your story. _____

_____

2. Where and when does the story take place? _____

_____

3. How did you become enchanted? _____

_____

4. When did you realize you were enchanted? _____

_____

5. Describe how the spell got you in trouble. _____

_____

_____

_____

6. How did you manage to break the spell? _____

_____

_____

Weird, Strange, and Unbelievable

1.93 Me—Home Alone

Directions: Imagine being home alone at night and hearing strange, frightening sounds. Answer the questions and write a story about being home alone. Create interesting characters, an exciting plot, and a climax for your story.

1. When were you home alone? _____

2. Why were you home alone? _____

3. What were you doing when you first heard the strange, frightening

   sounds? _____

   _____

4. Where did the sounds come from? _____

5. Describe the sounds. _____

   _____

6. Describe your feelings when you heard the sounds. _____

   _____

7. What did you do after hearing the sounds? _____

   _____

8. Did you find out what was making the sounds? Explain. _____

   _____

   _____

Name _____ Date _____

1.94 A Big Switch

Directions: Imagine that you could switch places with a plant or an animal for a day. You would become that plant or animal for twenty-four hours. Answer the questions and write a story about your experience. Create interesting characters, an exciting plot, and a climax for your story.

1. What plant or animal would you switch places with? Why? _____

_____

_____

2. Where would you be after switching places? _____

_____

3. Describe your "new" self. _____

_____

_____

4. Describe what you would see, hear, feel, smell, and taste. _____

_____

_____

_____

5. What would be the strangest thing about switching places?

_____

_____

_____

Weird, Strange, and Unbelievable

1.95 Super Running Shoes

Weird, Strange, and Unbelievable

Directions: Imagine that you were given a pair of running shoes that made you the fastest runner in the world. Answer the questions and write a story about these super running shoes. Create interesting characters, an exciting plot, and a climax for your story.

1. Name and describe the characters in your story. _____

_____

2. Where and when does this story take place? _____

_____

3. Who gave you the running shoes? _____

4. Why did this person give them to you? _____

_____

5. How did you discover their super speed? _____

_____

6. What did you do after you learned about their speed? _____

_____

_____

7. What eventually happened to the super running shoes? _____

_____

_____

1.96 Back to the Past

Directions: Imagine being able to go back to last year knowing everything you know now. Answer the questions and write a story about returning to the past. Create interesting characters, an exciting plot, and a climax for your story.

1. Name and describe the main characters of your story. _____

_____

2. How do you return to the past? _____

_____

3. Describe the past you return to. _____

_____

_____

4. Knowing the things you know now, would you change anything in the past? If yes, what? If no, why not? _____

_____

_____

5. Would any changes you made in the past change the present? Explain.

_____

_____

_____

Weird, Strange, and Unbelievable

1.97 Talking Teddy

Directions: Imagine a teddy bear, or another stuffed animal, suddenly beginning to talk. Answer the questions and write a story about this talking stuffed animal. Create interesting characters, an exciting plot, and a climax for your story.

1. Describe the stuffed animal. _____

_____

2. When does it begin to talk? _____

3. Why does it begin to talk? _____

_____

4. What does it say? _____

_____

5. What do you do when it begins to talk? _____

_____

6. Does anyone else know the stuffed animal can talk? _____

7. Do you tell anyone about the talking stuffed animal? Explain. _____

_____

8. Does the stuffed animal eventually stop talking? Explain. _____

_____

1.98 Fantasy Pet

Directions: Imagine being able to have a fantasy pet—for example, a dragon, a unicorn, or a giant eagle you can fly on. Answer the questions and write a story about your fantasy pet. Create interesting characters, an exciting plot, and a climax for your story.

1. Name and describe your fantasy pet. _____

_____

_____

2. Name and describe the main characters in your story. _____

_____

_____

3. Where and when does the story take place? _____

_____

4. How did you get your fantasy pet? _____

_____

_____

5. What do you and your fantasy pet do together? _____

_____

_____

_____

_____

Weird, Strange, and Unbelievable

1.99 Ancient Artifact

Directions: An *artifact* is an object produced long ago. For example, it might be a very old coin, tool, or ring. Imagine that you are exploring a cave and you find an ancient artifact. Answer the questions; then write a story about this artifact and its special powers. Create interesting characters, an exciting plot, and a climax for your story.

1. Name and describe the main characters in your story. _____

_____

2. Where and when does this story take place? _____

_____

3. Describe the artifact you find. _____

_____

4. What are its special powers? _____

_____

5. How do you learn of these powers? _____

_____

6. What happens after you learn of its powers? _____

_____

7. Do you keep the artifact? Or do you return it to the cave so that no one

   else can find it? Explain. _____

_____

1.100 Invisible Me

Directions: Imagine that you gain the power to make yourself invisible. But this power lasts only a day. Answer the questions and write a story about when you were invisible. Create interesting characters, an exciting plot, and a climax for your story.

1. Name and describe the main characters in your story. _____

_____

2. Where and when does this story take place? _____

_____

3. How do you gain the power to become invisible? _____

_____

4. How do you feel when you are invisible? _____

_____

5. Describe what you do when you are invisible. _____

_____

_____

6. Does anyone know about your power? Explain. _____

_____

7. What happens when your power begins to weaken? _____

_____

Weird, Strange, and Unbelievable

PART 2

Writing the Draft

Writing the draft is the part of the writing process in which ideas are put into words. For many students, this is a hard and frustrating task. It is the real work of writing.

Expressing ideas is a big step beyond conceiving ideas, and even the most capable students often need encouragement and guidance to articulate their thoughts and fashion them into a clearly written piece. To help your students approach their drafts with confidence, explain that a first draft is only the first attempt of what may turn out to be many attempts at completing a piece. Few writers get a draft "right" the first time, or the second, or the third. It is not uncommon for professional authors to work through a dozen or more drafts, and even then they may not be fully satisfied that they expressed their ideas in the best way possible. A draft should be considered as but one step forward in the process of finishing a piece.

For many writers the draft is a time of discovery. Some drafts closely follow the ideas that the writer has already formulated; others lead the writer to new ideas. Some are written quickly with high energy and emotion; others are written in a series of starts and stops because the writer has trouble finding his way. Some surprise the writer with unexpected insights; others are disappointing and force the writer to return to his original ideas to figure out what is wrong. Throughout all this, it is the writer's decisions that ultimately guide the development of the draft.

Students should look at a draft as a testing ground where they can examine their ideas and decide if they are writing exactly what they wish to say. I once had a student who expressed frustration that he had to write four drafts of a story before he was satisfied he had expressed his ideas the best he could. I explained that writing the first three drafts was the only way he could have gotten to the fourth. Rather than viewing reworked drafts as failures, writers should see each draft as an opportunity that leads them closer to the clear expression of ideas.

Without question, writing a draft is work. You can, however, make writing drafts easier for your students by teaching them the basics of composition. Even young students can benefit from understanding the fundamentals of sentences, paragraphs, and good writing.

Sentences: The Foundation of the Draft

To write with competence, students must have a basic knowledge and understanding of sentences. For students in the elementary grades, this understanding must include the four types of sentences—*declarative, interrogative, imperative,* and *exclamatory*—as well as *simple, compound,* and *complex* sentence structures. Understanding sentence types and structures will help them to write with proficiency and variety.

Exercise 2.1 Types of Sentences

Write the following sample sentences on an overhead projector or the board:

- Rashad walked to school. (declarative)
- Did Susan finish her homework? (interrogative)
- Close the window. (imperative)
- Watch out! (exclamatory)

Discuss each of the four types of sentences and point out the end punctuation. A *declarative* sentence is a statement and requires a period. An *interrogative* sentence is a question and requires a question mark. An *imperative* sentence is a command or request and requires a period. An *exclamatory* sentence expresses great emotion and requires an exclamation point.

Next, explain that a sentence must contain a *subject* and a *predicate* to express a complete thought. Note the subject and predicate in each of the examples. In the declarative sentence, *Rashad* is the subject and *walked* is the predicate. In the interrogative sentence, *Susan* is the subject and *did finish* is the predicate. In the imperative sentence, *close* is the predicate and the subject is understood to be *you*, the person to whom the command is directed. *You* (understood) is also the subject of the exclamatory sentence, in which *watch* is the predicate.

After discussing the examples, ask students to volunteer other examples of each type of sentence. Write the examples on the overhead projector or the board and identify the subjects and predicates of the sentences.

Exercise 2.2 Sentence Structures

Write the following examples of sentence structures on an overhead projector or the board:

- Maria plays the flute in the school band. (simple)
- Sam enjoys sports, but his sister loves music. (compound)
- Whenever it snows, Will goes snowboarding. (complex)

Explain that the examples are three common sentence structures. (The compound-complex sentence is a fourth structure, but it is not a part of the typical fourth- and fifth-grade language arts curriculum and is not addressed here.) Understanding these structures will help students to use different forms of sentences in their writing. Of course, the amount of information about sentences you provide to your students should be based on their abilities and needs. Advanced students will benefit from more details—for example, direct and indirect objects—while for some students, simply realizing there are different kinds of sentences will help them to vary their writing.

The first example is a simple sentence. It has one subject, *Maria*, and one predicate, *plays*.

The second example is a compound sentence. In a compound sentence, two separate sentences are connected with the words *and*, *but*, *or*, or *nor*. Note the subject, *Sam*, and the predicate, *enjoys*, in the first sentence, and the subject, *sister*, and the predicate, *loves*, in the second. Also note that *but* is the connecting word.

The third example is a complex sentence. A complex sentence has one independent clause, which can stand alone as a simple sentence, and one dependent clause, which cannot. In the example, *whenever it snows* is the dependent clause, and *Will goes snowboarding* is the independent clause. (Note: Independent clauses are also called main clauses, and dependent clauses are also called subordinate clauses.)

Emphasize to your students that by using all three forms of sentences they will be able to vary their writing and present their ideas in an interesting manner. Ask volunteers to offer examples of each form of sentence. Write their examples on an overhead projector or the board and discuss them, making sure that everyone can identify each of the three forms. For additional practice with sentences, assign Worksheets 2.1 and 2.2 at the end of this section.

Exercise 2.3 Combining and Varying Sentences

Write these examples on an overhead projector or the board:

> *After school Ashley did her homework. She went shopping with her mother. She went to dance practice.*

Explain that these three simple sentences, although written correctly, are flat and boring. Imagine a whole article or story written like this. Short sentences like these can be combined to make writing smoother and more interesting, as in the following example:

> *After school Ashley did her homework, went shopping with her mother, and went to dance practice.*

Now offer this example:

The night sky darkened. The stars appeared and began to twinkle.

Explain that these sentences can be combined and rewritten slightly, but with the result showing a noteworthy difference:

As the night sky darkened, the stars appeared and began to twinkle.

Emphasize that combining and varying sentences makes writing more interesting and showcases ideas for readers. For additional practice, assign Worksheets 2.3 and 2.4 at the end of this section.

Building Paragraphs

A well-written paragraph is constructed of sentences related to one main idea. The paragraph contains a topic sentence, which states the main idea of the paragraph, and other sentences that support the main idea with details and examples.

Although the topic sentence is the first sentence in most paragraphs, it may appear in the middle or at the end. For most young writers, placing the topic sentence at the beginning of the paragraph makes it easier to organize the paragraph and provide supporting details.

Paragraphs may vary in length, depending on their main idea and supporting details. When students ask you how long a paragraph should be (and they will), say that a paragraph must be long enough to fully develop its main idea.

A major problem with the paragraphs of many young writers is insufficient development. Students often use general or vague main ideas or supporting ideas that lack specific details. Encourage your students to develop their paragraphs one sentence at a time, starting with the topic sentence, which they must then support with details and examples.

Exercise 2.4 Constructing Paragraphs

Write this example of an obviously undeveloped paragraph on an overhead projector or the board:

The movie was great. It was the best movie I ever saw.

Explain that although it is clear the writer liked the movie, he or she offers no supporting details. The absence of supporting ideas undermines the main idea. Ask your students what kinds of details could be included that would support and strengthen the main idea in this paragraph. Write their suggestions down and discuss them, noting how they could support the main idea. Possible details include the following:

- The title of the movie
- The type of movie
- The actors and actresses and how they helped to make the movie great
- A brief description of the plot and how it helped to make the movie great
- Why the author liked the movie

Exercise 2.5 Reviewing Paragraphs

From your students' reading book, or their science or social studies text, choose two or three descriptive paragraphs. (Descriptive paragraphs are best for this exercise because they include details.) Have your students read the paragraphs. For each one, identify the main idea, find the topic sentence, and discuss the supporting details. Direct the attention of your students to the construction of the paragraph, particularly how details support and expand the main idea.

Encourage your students to concentrate on building solid paragraphs in their writing. Remind them to organize each paragraph around a main idea, express that idea in a topic sentence, and provide supporting details. For additional practice with paragraphs, assign Worksheets 2.5, 2.6, and 2.7 at the end of this section.

Showing and Not Telling

Good writers understand that they must show and not tell about ideas if their writing is to have the greatest impact. Because showing requires action, authors who show, and avoid merely telling, write with sharper and clearer imagery. The difference between telling about an idea and showing the idea through action can be significant.

Exercise 2.6 Show, Show, Show

To illustrate to your students the power of showing over telling, write this example on an overhead projector or the board:

- When the toy broke, the little boy was upset. (telling)
- When the toy broke, the little boy stamped his foot and started to cry. (showing)

Explain that in the first sentence, the writer tells that the *boy was upset.* In the second sentence, however, *stamped his foot and started to cry* shows that the boy was upset. Showing provides action that the reader can visualize in her imagination, making the idea clear.

Now offer this example:

- The sunset was pretty. (telling)
- The sun drifted lower in the bright red sky. (showing)

The second sentence provides action—*The sun drifted lower*—and visual details—*in the bright red sky*—that enhance the idea of the sun setting. The second sentence is an example of stronger writing than the first.

Ask your students to volunteer additional examples that demonstrate showing and not telling. Write the examples on the overhead projector or the board and discuss the differences between showing and telling.

Encourage your students to show whenever possible and not merely tell. For more practice, assign Worksheet 2.8 at the end of this section.

Using Adjectives and Adverbs Wisely

Many students use too many adjectives and adverbs in their writing. Some overuse modifiers in a mistaken assumption that more details will make their writing better. The opposite is true. When overused, adjectives and adverbs weaken writing. Moreover, relying too heavily on adjectives and adverbs can cloud writing and distract the writer from choosing distinct nouns and strong verbs. Adjectives and adverbs should be used only when necessary.

Following are some examples I have come across in the writing of my students:

- the big red, white, and blue ball (This was a beach ball.)
- green grass (Unless the grass is dead or the season is winter, grass is green.)
- totally surprised (Can someone be partially surprised?)
- completely fooled (A person is either fooled or not fooled.)
- happy smile (Most smiles arise from happiness; the exception is a sad smile.)

When you teach adjectives and adverbs to your students, explain that while these words have a purpose in sentences, they should be chosen with care. Instead of bland modifiers, students should seek ones that provide sharp, distinct details.

To help your students gain an understanding and appreciation of the use of adjectives and adverbs, note examples in their reading. Point out how the proper use of adjectives or adverbs can enhance sentences. To provide your students with practice using adjectives and adverbs wisely in their writing, assign Worksheets 2.9, 2.10, and 2.11 at the end of this section.

Order and Sequence

In real life, things happen in order. All the things we do are part of a long (and sometimes complicated) sequence of cause and effect. In the same way, articles and stories must adhere to some form of order and sequence of events. Even stories that include flashbacks follow a plan of order.

For some students, the order in their writing resembles the order of a messy desk. The writing of these students can be hard to follow and certainly can be improved.

Problems with order usually arise from one of two causes: either the student is simply inattentive to order because he wants to finish the writing as fast as possible, or the student is so enthused with expressing his ideas that attention to order is lost. Whatever the reason, it must be corrected. Effective writing exhibits a sequential development of ideas in an ordered framework.

To help your students gain an understanding of order and sequence, discuss order and sequence in the stories and articles they read. Especially point out how ideas develop logically, how ideas are related, and how ideas are usually presented in sequence.

You should also encourage your students to concentrate on the order of ideas in their writing. Explain that for most pieces ideas should build logically from start to end. There are exceptions, of course, but for most young writers a chronological sequence provides a practical order. For students who have trouble maintaining a logical order in their writing, suggest that they write a list of their ideas according to time. Referring to their list as they write will help them to adhere to a consistent sequence. To provide students with practice on order and sequence, assign Worksheet 2.12 at the end of this section.

Using Active Constructions

Active constructions, sometimes referred to as *active voice*, help to make writing direct and strong. Passive constructions, also known as *passive voice*, make writing indirect and weak. Active constructions are clear and add force to writing. There is nothing vague or ambiguous about an active construction, as the following example shows:

- Jimmy finished his homework. (active)
- The homework was finished by Jimmy. (passive)

Notice that the active construction is shorter and provides a clear idea. The passive construction muddles along. In the active construction, *Jimmy* is the subject and *finished* is the predicate. There is no confusion that Jimmy finished the homework. In the passive construction, *homework* is the subject and the predicate is the phrase *was finished. Jimmy* becomes the object of the preposition *by*. Most readers easily understand the first sentence; some, however, have to think about the second. Active constructions are almost always a better choice than passive constructions because they help readers to visualize action and ideas.

Exercise 2.7 Active Versus Passive Constructions

Write the following example on an overhead projector or the board:

- Jamal hit a home run. (active)
- A home run was hit by Jamal. (passive)

Explain to your students the differences between active and passive constructions. Note that in the first sentence the action is clear. Although the second sentence says the same thing, the action is not expressed as clearly. Emphasize that this is the major difference between active and passive constructions: active constructions are clear and direct; passive constructions are wordy and less clear.

If necessary, offer this example:

- Larissa smiled at the baby. (active)
- The baby was smiled at by Larissa. (passive)

Ask your students which sentence they prefer. All (or at least most) should prefer the first, which is the active construction. For practice with active and passive constructions, assign Worksheet 2.13 at the end of this section.

Using Strong Verbs

Closely linked to active constructions are strong verbs. Like active constructions, strong verbs paint clear pictures in the imaginations of readers. English is a vast, rich language. We have words for just about everything, and we have precise verbs for all kinds of action. Encouraging your students to use precise action verbs in their writing will help them master this important writing technique.

Exercise 2.8 Strong Verbs

Write the following pairs of sentences on an overhead projector or the board:

- The wind was powerful.
- The wind gusted.

- The squirrel went up the tree.
- The squirrel scampered up the tree.

- The little girl called loudly for her brother.
- The little girl shouted for her brother.

Explain that the second sentence of each pair uses a strong verb to show the action. Strong verbs result in writing that is less wordy, particularly in cases where adverbs are used to support a verb's action. For practice with strong verbs, assign Worksheet 2.14 at the end of this section.

Verb Tenses

The tense of a verb shows when something happens, or happened, in a sentence. The three most commonly used tenses are *present*, *past*, and *future*. Although other tenses include present perfect, past perfect, and future perfect, most students in fourth and fifth grade simply use present, past, and future.

Explain to your students what each tense shows:

- Verbs in the present tense show action that is happening now. For example, *Sandra walks to school each day.*
- Verbs in the past tense show action that has happened. *Sandra walked to school yesterday.*
- Verbs in the future tense show action that will happen. *Sandra will walk to school tomorrow.*

Explain to your students that most writers use the past tense, because the events they are writing about have already happened. This is especially true for stories and most articles. In some articles, however—for example, essays and editorials—an author may want to convey a feeling that the subject of the article is currently happening. In such cases, the author uses present tense.

As you discuss tenses with your students, note that they must choose the correct tense for the stories and articles they write. A narrative, for example, based on a past event, requires the past tense. An article about the lunches currently served in the school cafeteria would probably best be written in the present tense.

Once a tense is chosen, consistency is essential. Encourage your students to pay close attention to the tenses they use to avoid shifting tenses unnecessarily. I have read pieces in which students start in the past tense, then switch to the present, only to switch back to the past. Tense shifts often occur when students write action scenes in stories. They become so involved with the action, which in their imaginations is immediate, that they inadvertently switch to present tense. Once the action scene is done, they return to the past.

Selecting an inappropriate tense for writing and unnecessarily shifting tenses prove to be confusing for readers. Tense shifts can undermine expression and obscure ideas. For practice with verb tenses, assign Worksheet 2.15 at the end of this section.

Subject-Verb Agreement

A subject and verb of a sentence must always agree. In the present tense, singular subjects require the singular form of verbs, and plural subjects require the plural form of verbs. Agreement is not an issue for sentences in the past tense, because in the past tense the forms of verbs are the same for singular and plural subjects. The only exception is the verb *be*, for which the singular past tense form is *was* and the plural past tense form is *were*.

Exercise 2.9 Agreement

On an overhead projector or the board, write these examples:

- Tim walks to school each day.
- Tim and Sancho walk to school each day.
- Tim walked to school yesterday.
- Tim and Sancho walked to school yesterday.

Discuss the sentences and point out the subjects and verbs. Note that in the present tense, students must pay close attention to subject-verb agreement. In the present tense, the singular subject *Tim* requires the singular form of the verb *walk*, which is *walks*, and the plural subjects *Tim* and *Sancho* require the plural form, *walk*. When using the past tense, both singular and plural subjects use the same form, *walked*. For additional practice with subject-verb agreement, assign Worksheet 2.16 at the end of this section.

Point of View

Point of view (POV) is the way an author tells a story. The two most common points of view are the *first person point of view* and the *third person point of view*. Virtually all of your students will use these two points of view in their writing.

In the first person POV, the author is a participant in or observer of the action. The author tells the story or writes about an event or issue firsthand. The author refers to herself as "I." Students often find the first person POV easier to write with because they can use their own voice. It is also easier to write with emotion and feeling in the first person POV, because the writer assumes a role in the piece. The major disadvantage of this POV is the way in which it limits writing, especially for stories. The author, as participant in and narrator of the story, can write only about what she experiences in the story. For example, while writing in the first person POV, the author cannot describe the thoughts or feelings of another character (unless the author is telepathic).

In the third person POV, the author writes from a perspective outside the piece. The author is not a part of the action. Characters are referred to as "he" or "she."

The third person POV allows the author broader control of the piece, but the writing may not have the intimacy of a piece written in the first person. Most writing is done in the third person POV.

Probably the biggest problem young writers have with POV is consistency. Students may start a story in the first person, switch to the third, then switch back to the first, only to switch once again to the third. Rapid or unexpected switches between the first and third person POVs befuddle readers, and often confuse the writer as well. Stories and articles that suffer POV switches quickly lose focus. Ideas become muddled and writing loses direction.

To help your students gain an understanding of POV, discuss examples of POVs in their reading and explore why authors chose the POV they did. As your students learn to recognize POV in their reading, they will use POV effectively in their writing. For practice with POV, assign Worksheets 2.17 and 2.18 at the end of this section.

Comparison and Contrast

Comparing and *contrasting* are tools that enable writers to identify the similarities and differences between things. They allow writers to highlight details that evoke powerful images. Comparing and contrasting help to delineate ideas.

Explain to your students that comparing identifies similarities and that contrasting identifies differences. They should use comparison and contrast whenever they need to show how two things or ideas are alike and different.

Note that there are two methods for comparing and contrasting. In method one, the author describes the first idea fully, then describes the second fully, showing how they are alike and different. In method two, the author describes one feature of the first idea and compares and contrasts it to the same feature of the second idea. The author then compares and contrasts the second feature, then the third, and so on.

> ### Exercise 2.10 Comparing and Contrasting Pets
>
> **O**n an overhead projector or the board, write "cat" and "dog," or similar topics with which students are likely to be familiar. Explain to your students that the class is going to compare and contrast cats and dogs.
>
> Ask your students to volunteer ideas how cats and dogs are alike and different. Some similarities might include the following:
>
> - Both animals are mammals.
> - Both are popular as pets.
> - As pets they can become "members of the family."

Differences students might suggest include the following:

- Dogs are more playful; cats like to "do their own thing."
- Cats purr when contented; dogs wag their tails.
- Cats meow; dogs bark.

These are just some possibilities and it is likely your students will come up with more.

Suggest that students use comparing and contrasting in their own writing. For additional practice with comparison and contrast, assign Worksheet 2.19 at the end of this section.

Figurative Language

Figurative language can turn average writing into exceptional writing. Figures of speech include *similes*, *metaphors*, and *personification*.

Explain to your students that similes make comparisons using the words *like* or *as*. (*Than* can also be used in similes, but most fourth- and fifth-graders are more likely to use *like* or *as*.) Metaphors make comparisons without using *like* or *as*. Personification gives human qualities to nonhuman things and ideas. The great power of figurative language manifests in the enrichment of ideas.

Exercise 2.11 The Power of Figures of Speech

Write the following examples of figures of speech on an overhead projector or the board:

- The cat's eyes were like full moons in the darkness. (simile)
- The thief's stare was as cold as ice. (simile)
- The snow was a white blanket over the land. (metaphor)
- The trees fought the storm's winds. (personification)

Discuss each of the examples, and note how the comparison or personification is made. Also discuss how the figures of speech help readers visualize the idea expressed by the sentence. Ask your students to volunteer examples of similes, metaphors, and personifications. Write them down and discuss them, noting how the figures of speech enrich the ideas of the sentences. For more practice with figures of speech, assign Worksheet 2.20 at the end of this section.

Reproducible Worksheets

For many students, writing the draft is the most difficult part of the writing process. The worksheets included in this section are designed to give students practice in the techniques and strategies that make writing a draft easier. The skills covered on the worksheets are the foundation of proficient writing. Encourage your students to incorporate these skills in their writing.

The worksheets that follow are linked to the teaching suggestions of this section. The Answer Key offers possible answers to the worksheets. While each worksheet stands alone and can be assigned with little or no introduction, the worksheets will be most effective if you offer instruction and guidance on the skills presented. Once the skills have been taught, reinforce them through the revision process that is described in Part 3.

2.1 Kinds of Sentences

Directions: Follow the instructions below and write examples of the four kinds of sentences. Be sure to use correct end punctuation.

1. Write a declarative sentence using each of the following.

A. puppy _____

_____

B. clouds _____

_____

2. Write an interrogative sentence using each of the following.

A. homework _____

_____

B. lunch _____

_____

3. Write an imperative sentence using each of the following.

A. window _____

_____

B. room _____

_____

4. Write an exclamatory sentence using each of the following.

A. car _____

_____

B. ice _____

_____

Writing the Draft

2.2 Expanding Sentences

Directions: Use the phrases at the bottom of the page to expand each simple sentence. (Some sentences can be expanded with more than one phrase.)

1. The dog barked . . . _____

2. Tom slipped . . . _____

3. Brianna almost cried . . . _____

4. The little girl waited . . . _____

5. The thunder rumbled . . . _____

6. Paulo smiled . . . _____

7. Lila practiced . . . _____

8. The river flooded . . . _____

Phrases

the flute each night
inside the house
in pain
when she stubbed her toe
on the icy sidewalk
through the night
for her grandparents to come

because of the heavy rain
during the storm
after dinner
after finishing the test
at the thought of no homework
in relief

2.3 Combining Sentences

Directions: Use *and*, *but*, or *or* to combine and rewrite each pair of sentences.

1. Carl came home from school. He did his homework. _____

_____

2. It snowed all night. School was canceled. _____

_____

3. Susan likes to dance. Staci, her sister, likes to sing. _____

_____

4. The clouds grew darker. The wind began to gust. _____

_____

5. Amanda enjoys basketball. She enjoys softball too. _____

_____

6. It might rain tonight. It might snow. _____

_____

7. Tom could do his math homework. He could work on his science project.

_____

8. The puppy growled at the toy. It was a playful growl. _____

_____

2.4 Varying Sentences

Directions: Rewrite each sentence. Use the given word or phrase to vary the form of the sentence. The first one is done as an example.

1. The sun set and daylight faded. (as) _As the sun set, daylight faded._

2. Luis finished his homework and then watched TV. (after) _____

_____

3. It rained all night, and the river was rising. (because) _____

_____

4. The computer crashed, and Rashad was almost done with his science project. (when) _____

5. Carla had a terrible cold, but she still went to dance practice. (even though) _____

6. The rain ended, and the sky quickly cleared. (once) _____

_____

7. It was raining, and Trish finished reading *Charlotte's Web*. (while) _____

_____

8. It was the worst part of the storm, and lightning flashed and thunder exploded. (during) _____

_____

Writing the Draft

2.5 Understanding Paragraphs

Directions: Read the article below. It should be written in five paragraphs. Place the symbol L before the first word that starts each paragraph. Explain your reasons for marking the paragraphs on the lines at the bottom of the page.

Do you know the difference between *meteoroid*, *meteor*, and *meteorite*? Many people find these words confusing. Meteoroids are chunks of rock or metal that speed through space. Some are very large and may be hundreds of feet wide. Others may be the size of a small stone. Most meteoroids orbit the sun. Sometimes a meteoroid will enter the Earth's atmosphere. Friction with the atmosphere will cause it to heat up and burn. When a meteoroid begins to burn in the atmosphere, it leaves a streak of light. This is called a meteor, or shooting star. Most meteors burn up before they hit the ground. If a meteor does not burn completely, it will hit the Earth. A meteor that hits the Earth is called a meteorite. If a meteor is big, this will cause a great explosion and much destruction. Most meteoroids stay safely away from the Earth. Of those that enter the atmosphere, most burn up long before reaching the ground.

_____

_____

_____

_____

_____

_____

_____

_____

_____

Writing the Draft

2.6 Writing Topic Sentences

Directions: Read each paragraph. Write a topic sentence for each one. Then answer the question at the bottom of the sheet.

1. _____
Although he reads many different kinds of books, Dan likes science fiction the best. He enjoys reading about how people might one day travel to the stars.

2. _____
She stars on her school's soccer, basketball, and softball teams. She also is a fast runner and swimmer. In fact, Jenna is great at every sport she has ever tried.

3. _____
He looked at all the books piled on his desk. His math book, history book, science text, and language arts folder were waiting for him. Bradley didn't know where to begin. But he knew that if he was to finish his homework tonight, he had better start soon.

4. _____
First she looked in the kitchen drawer. That was where she usually put her keys. They weren't there. Next Christy checked her jacket pocket. They weren't there either. Then she searched her room. About to give up, she remembered—her knapsack.

5. Choose one of the paragraphs. Explain what clues helped you to decide on the topic sentence. _____

_____

_____

_____

Writing the Draft

2.7 Writing Supporting Details

Directions: Write at least three supporting details for each topic sentence.

1. Carlita knew there was much to do to get ready for the birthday party.

_____

_____

_____

2. As the storm approached, the sky darkened.

_____

_____

_____

3. Marc enjoyed helping his father around the house.

_____

_____

_____

4. It was the worst heat wave in years.

_____

_____

_____

Writing the Draft

2.8 Showing and Not Telling

Directions: Rewrite each sentence to *show* the action and not *tell* about it. The first one is done as an example.

1. Sara was a good student. _The first thing Sara did when she got home from school was to begin her homework._

2. It was a bad storm. _____

_____

3. The puppy was playful. _____

_____

4. Kevin was the winner of the fifth-grade race. _____

_____

5. The winds of the storm were powerful. _____

_____

6. Jess was scared by the strange noises. _____

_____

7. Miguel is an excellent baseball player. _____

_____

8. It snowed heavily. _____

_____

Writing the Draft

2.9 Choosing Adjectives

Directions: Complete each sentence by filling in the blank with an adjective. Use adjectives that help to paint a picture in the reader's imagination. Choose adjectives from the list below. (Not all of the adjectives will be used.)

1. The _____ sun baked the land with heat.

2. Everyone listened as the _____ guide told the _____ story of the ghost wind.

3. Shari looked at the _____ pile of books on her desk.

4. A _____ porch surrounded the _____ house.

5. _____ roses were at the center of the _____ garden.

6. The _____ puppy bounded across the room after the _____ ball.

7. Josh enjoys playing _____ video games.

8. The _____ mountains rose into the _____ sky.

9. As he walked to school, Tim pulled up his collar to block the _____ wind.

10. The wolf's _____ howl filled the _____ woods.

Adjectives

red	tiny	icy	playful	blazing	beautiful
lonely	chilling	blue	old	stately	silly
huge	tall	spongy	exciting	great	empty

Writing the Draft

2.10 Choosing Adverbs

Directions: Complete each sentence by filling in the blanks with an adverb. Choose adverbs from the list below. (Not all of the adverbs will be used.)

1. The little boy believed the story _____.

2. _____ it would be time to leave.

3. Tara _____ updated her computer with new software.

4. The leaves rustled _____ in the light breeze.

5. Travis studied _____ for the history test.

6. Before giving her speech, Kim practiced it _____.

7. James _____ finishes his homework on time.

8. Not wanting to miss the start of the game, Michael ate his dinner

   _____.

9. Vanessa likes numbers and finishes her math homework _____.

10. Jon read the directions _____ and got several problems wrong.

Adverbs

recently	often	soon	carelessly	hard
clearly	usually	softly	very	easily
completely	personally	quickly	carefully	loudly

Writing the Draft

2.11 Writing Descriptions

Directions: Choose a place or thing. For example, this might be the street in front of your home, a big tree in your backyard, or a shopping mall. Think of your senses and list words that describe this place or thing. Then write a descriptive paragraph about this place or thing.

1. Place or thing: _____

2. Sight words: _____

3. Sound words: _____

4. Touch words: _____

5. Smell words: _____

6. Taste words: _____

7. Paragraph: _____

_____

_____

_____

_____

_____

_____

_____

Writing the Draft

2.12 Understanding the Order of Ideas

Directions: Each set of sentences below belongs to a paragraph. But the sentences are out of order and do not follow one another correctly. Rewrite each of the paragraphs so that the ideas are in order. Use a separate sheet of paper.

1. She could not stop fussing. She took a deep breath and walked toward the piano at the front of the room. Jill was nervous. When her piano instructor called her name, Jill stood. But she still felt nervous. When her mother tried to assure her that she would do fine, Jill smiled. This was her first piano recital, and she was afraid she would make mistakes.

2. He knew it was going to be a busy day. After dinner Alvaro went online to find information for his science report. He came back from practice around four P.M. He watched his little brother until dinner, because his parents went shopping. That morning, he helped his father clean the garage. By the time Alvaro went to sleep that night, he was very tired. In the afternoon Alvaro went to soccer practice. Alvaro woke up early on Saturday.

Writing the Draft

2.13 Using Active Constructions

Directions: Each sentence is a passive construction. Rewrite each to make it an active construction. The first one is done as an example.

1. The ball was hit by Robbie. *Robbie hit the ball.* _____

2. The kite was whipped about by the wind. _____

_____

3. The dishes were washed by Eduardo. _____

_____

4. The speech was given by Gina. _____

_____

5. The cover for the class magazine was designed by Clare. _____

_____

6. A solo in the fifth-grade concert was sung by Carlos. _____

_____

7. The bird was sneaked up on by the cat. _____

_____

8. Dangerous driving conditions were caused by the storm. _____

_____

Writing the Draft

2.14 Using Strong Verbs

Directions: Each sentence below uses a weak verb and an adverb to show action. Rewrite the sentences. Use the strong verbs at the bottom of the page that do not need the help of adverbs. The first one is done as an example. (Not all of the verbs will be used.)

1. The fox walked sneakily toward the chicken coop. _The fox crept toward the chicken coop._

2. The little girl spoke softly during the movie. _____

_____

3. Tommy cried loudly when his toy broke. _____

_____

4. The eagle flew gracefully over the valley. _____

_____

5. Jason moved quickly out of the ball's way. _____

_____

6. Melissa went across the room quietly. _____

_____

Writing the Draft

Strong Verbs

whispered	tiptoed	pounced	raced	laughed
dodged	soared	crashed	screamed	crept

2.15 Using Verb Tenses Correctly

Directions: Identify whether each of the following sentences is written in the present tense, past tense, or future tense.

1. Liz walked to school with Heather this morning. _____

2. Michael is a good student and a good athlete. _____

3. Alyssa watches her little brother each day after school. _____

4. The magician will be the last act in the show. _____

5. The old dog played like he was still a puppy. _____

6. Roberto will study for his science test after dinner. _____

Directions: Write three sentences of your own. Write one in the present tense, another in the past tense, and the third in the future tense.

1. _____

_____

2. _____

_____

3. _____

_____

Writing the Draft

2.16 Subject-Verb Agreement

Directions: Complete each sentence by writing the correct form of a verb. Choose from the verbs at the bottom of the page. Each verb should be used only once. (Remember to use the correct form.)

1. Tara _____ chocolate ice cream.

2. Wil and Raymondo _____ baseball every day in the summer.

3. Most children _____ playing computer games.

4. Erin _____ her flute every evening.

5. A squirrel _____ in the big tree in our backyard.

6. The Smith twins _____ exactly alike.

7. Tina _____ her little sister with homework.

8. Each day birds _____ to the bird feeder in my yard.

9. The flowers _____ Aunt Janet's garden with color.

10. Antonio _____ hard for every test.

Verbs

| play | fill | enjoy | study | help |
| look | come | like | live | practice |

2.17 First Person Point of View

Directions: Rewrite the story from the third person point of view to the first person point of view. Pay close attention to the use of pronouns.

Samier sighed, thinking of all the homework he had. He did not know where to begin.

He looked at the pile of books on his desk. He knew he had better start if he wanted to meet his friends later.

Samier opened his math book first. After he finished ten division problems, he did his spelling. Next he did his history.

Finished at last, Samier went to see his friends. They were waiting for him at the basketball court.

As soon as Samier got there, they chose teams and started a game.

_____

_____

_____

_____

_____

_____

_____

_____

_____

_____

_____

_____

Writing the Draft

2.18 Third Person Point of View

Directions: Rewrite the story from the first person point of view to the third person point of view. Pay close attention to the use of pronouns.

Too excited to sleep, I woke up early. This was the day my father and I were going on a ten-kilometer bike tour. The goal of the tour was to raise money for charity. I thought it would be a great day.

By the time the tour began, I wasn't so sure. The sky had grown dark and a cool wind was blowing. I was worried that it would rain.

All the time we rode, I kept looking at the sky. Just as we came to the finish line, the first drops started to fall on us.

I smiled. It had been a great day after all.

_____

_____

_____

_____

_____

_____

_____

_____

_____

_____

_____

Writing the Draft

2.19 Comparison and Contrast

Directions: Read the article about African elephants and Indian elephants. List how they are alike and different.

The elephant is the largest living land mammal on Earth. There are two species of elephants: the African elephant and the Indian elephant. Both elephants have trunks and eat grass and leaves. But there are important differences, too.

The African elephant is found mostly in the tropical forests and grasslands of Africa. It is the bigger of the two kinds of elephants and can reach a height of thirteen feet. The African elephant also has larger ears. From the top to the bottom, an African elephant's ears may reach a length of five feet.

The Indian elephant is found mostly in India and Southeast Asia. It is usually smaller than the African elephant, but it is taller at the arch of the back.

Compare
How the African elephant and Indian elephant are alike:

_____

_____

_____

_____

Contrast
How the African elephant and Indian elephant are different:

_____

_____

_____

_____

_____

Writing the Draft

2.20 Figures of Speech

1. The hawk soared like a(n) _____ in the sky. _____

2. The moment the race began, Jared ran as fast as a(n) _____ toward the finish line. _____

3. The giant was a(n) _____. _____

4. The burglar sneaked around the house like a(n) _____. _____

5. The shark was a(n) _____ streaking for its target. _____

6. The sound of the smoke detector was a(n) _____ that woke everyone up. _____

Write a sentence that shows personification for each of the following.

7. The sky _____

_____

8. The flowers _____

_____

9. The fireflies _____

_____

Writing the Draft

Revision

R evision is the stage of the writing process where an author reworks, refines, and finalizes her ideas. It is a time of "re-seeing" what she has written and making it better.

Revision is essential for improving writing, yet students often resist revision. They may feel that once they have finished the draft the writing is done; they may believe that they have written their best on the draft; or they may be unsure of how to revise. But effective revision is critical for making writing as clear and meaningful to readers as possible. For most authors, it is solid revision that leads to the successful expression of ideas.

What Is Revision?

In its broadest sense, revision includes any activity that makes a draft better. In its narrowest, it is replacing one word with another because the second word better communicates what the author wants to say. Note that editing of mechanics—capitalization and punctuation, for example—also occurs during revision. However, revision should not be confused with proofreading, the primary purpose of which is to correct errors in mechanics (see Part 4, Proofreading).

Revision includes a variety of activities. As your students revise their writing, they may be engaged in any of the following:

- Rereading
- Rewriting
- Reviewing
- Rethinking
- Rearranging
- Restructuring
- Tightening
- Deleting
- Moving

147

- Expanding
- Unifying
- Correcting
- Redrafting

When you introduce revision to your students, explain that writing is not finished until it has been revised. Emphasize that all professional writers revise their work. You might mention this tidbit about Ernest Hemingway: during an interview for the *Paris Review*, Hemingway said that he rewrote the last page of his book *A Farewell to Arms* thirty-nine times before he was satisfied with his work. Undoubtedly the eyes of many of your students will widen at that, and you might want to assure them that you do not expect them to revise their work so extensively, but it does illustrate the seriousness with which professional authors undertake the task of revision. Professional authors know that their best writing takes form during revision.

Nurturing Skills in Revision

Revision is detailed, demanding work. Not only must the writer work to improve specifics—for example, select the best words to express an idea clearly and smoothly—he must also work to improve the piece as a whole. Moreover, each piece is different and has different strengths and weaknesses.

Although just about every article or story benefits from revision, the amount and type of revision vary. Some pieces require extensive revision. Maybe the writer drifted off the topic, maybe she did not provide enough information to explain her ideas, or maybe her organization was weak. In other cases, a piece might require only some tightening and minor rewriting. Emphasize that the author's initial task during revision is to recognize what needs to be reworked and what does not.

Being able to recognize what needs to be revised requires a grasp of the fundamentals of effective writing (which were discussed in Part 2, Writing the Draft). The following elements are essential to any piece and will provide your students with direction as they revise their writing. Depending on the abilities of your students, you might find it useful to review these elements in some detail:

- Basic structure of opening, body, and closing
- Paragraphs
- Main ideas and details
- Order and sequence
- Varying sentence structure
- Subject-verb agreement
- Active constructions
- Strong verbs
- Showing and not telling

- Consistent tenses
- Consistent point of view
- Figurative language

When teaching revision, base your expectations for revision only on skills that you have taught. Focus on one or two skills at a time, because addressing too many at once can be overwhelming to students. You must also adjust your instruction to the level and abilities of your students. Use terminology your students understand. Avoid words like *obscure* and *vague* if such words are not a part of your students' vocabularies. Instead, offer clear suggestions and comments that address specific weaknesses.

For many students, revision can be both puzzling and frustrating. Many work hard on a draft but do not know how they can make it better. They need guidance and encouragement.

Although you should offer as much guidance and encouragement as you can for revision, be mindful not to revise for your students. Sometimes students will be stumped in trying to revise a part of their writing. They will ask you for help. When they do, avoid making the changes for them. You can offer suggestions, for example, "How else might you say this?" or "What more do you think your readers will want to know about this?" or "How might you make this more clear?" But leave the actual changes to your students. Revision is an individual process, based on the writer's purpose for the piece. Thus, decisions for revision are the responsibility of the author.

Plan for Revision

Because revision encompasses so many elements, there is no firm, set procedure for revising one's writing. As they gain experience with revision, most writers eventually develop their own methods. Practice leads to proficiency, but until they master the skills necessary for effective revision, your students will benefit from your instruction and support.

To help your students with their revision efforts, encourage them to start revising from the perspective of the overall piece and work down to the details. This plan provides direction and helps students to focus on specific elements at different points in the revision process.

Instruct your students to begin by reading through the entire piece and concentrating on unity. *Unity* is a broad term that can be used to include virtually all aspects of a piece, but for young writers it may be limited to refer to topic and purpose. In an article that demonstrates unity, all main ideas and supporting details relate to the topic. All parts of the piece are essential to the whole. Everything moves the piece forward in support of the author's purpose. For example, an article about how to train a puppy that also includes information about kittens would suffer from a lack of unity. It would prove to be confusing to readers, who expect to read about puppies and not kittens. To achieve unity, any material not important to the topic should be deleted.

After making certain that all parts of their writing belong and that the piece shows unity, students should read through their piece again and concentrate on general consistency. Young writers should particularly focus on structure, tense, and point of view.

The overall structure of the piece should be logical. There should be a solid opening, logical development through the body, and a strong closing. Main ideas should be supported with details and examples.

All tenses should be consistent and appropriate. For example, a story should be written in the past tense. An essay, however, might best be written in the present. Any unnecessary shifts in tense should be corrected.

Point of view must be consistent as well. If a story is started in the first person point of view, it should continue in the first person. Likewise, if a story is begun in the third person point of view, it should remain in the third person. Switching from first to third person point of view weakens a piece and undermines the author's control of the material.

Next, encourage your students to focus on paragraphs, sentences, and words. Again, they should eliminate anything that does not belong. They should also strive to ensure that every expository paragraph has a topic sentence and sufficient details. In addition, encourage students to vary and combine sentences, make certain that subjects and verbs agree, use active constructions, and select just the right words to express their ideas. Now is the time to make writing the best it can be.

As most students gain experience and confidence in revision, they will revise weaknesses as they go along, addressing various elements of their writing simultaneously. They will come to see revision as a satisfying part of the writing process, because it enables them to make certain that their writing expresses exactly what they wish to say.

Exercise 3.1 Recognizing Good Writing

Recognizing good writing is a major step in revising one's own writing. Use well-written articles and stories from your students' texts as examples, and discuss why these pieces may be viewed as samples of good writing. Read the material and note the unity—how everything in the article or story relates to the topic and the author's purpose. Note the organization of the piece and how the structure displays ideas in a logical manner. Point out the use of consistent tenses and point of view. Examine how the author varied his sentences, used active constructions, relied on strong verbs, and achieved a smooth flow of ideas.

Good writing is almost always a result of good revision. Emphasize that revision is an author's opportunity to make her writing as clear and interesting as possible for her readers. This is the time to put ideas into their final shape.

Revision Peer Consultants

One of the most maddening aspects of revision for students is writing that is not wrong, but that could be improved. I once had a student ask me, "How do you know when to stop revising?" This was an excellent question, for which the only answer is, "When you are convinced the material is as strong and clear as you can make it." This, of course, is not the answer students want. Most prefer a simple explanation that tells them when revision is done.

Many students find revision to be a hard part of the writing process because they are not sure what they should revise. It is difficult for young authors to step far enough back from their writing to be objective and see the weaknesses in their material.

Sometimes consulting with a partner can help. Partners can read each other's work and offer suggestions for revision. The partners do not correct the papers. Instead they underline items they feel should be revised and write comments in the margins. The author can then consider the places his partner identified for revision.

When you organize your students into consulting partners, try to pair students who will work well together. For example, best friends, who might have too many things to talk about other than writing, usually do not make a good combination. Another example of a potentially troublesome combination is matching a student who has low self-esteem with a student who has a strong personality. The dominant student might convince her tentative partner of the need to revise the entire paper even if it requires only minor rewriting.

Ideally, partners should have a separate space in which to work when consulting about writing. While a table in the back of the room is an excellent spot for consulting, in most classrooms pushing desks together is the norm. This arrangement will be satisfactory provided students work together quietly and efficiently.

When students are consulting, you should circulate around the room. Observe students, sit in on pairs as necessary, and offer suggestions of your own. However, be careful not to do the revising for your students. The more practice students have with revision, the more comfortable and confident they will become with the process.

Exercise 3.2 Revision Consultants

Divide your students into pairs. If you have an odd number of students in class, you may allow a team of three. Explain that partners are to act as peer revision consultants. Partners are to read each other's writing and identify instances where revision could improve the piece. Instruct your students to underline in pencil places on their partners' papers where revision might be helpful. Note that they should write brief comments in the adjacent margins. For example, a spot where two sentences could be combined might be identified and labeled "Combine sentences." After the partner (acting as a consultant) has written and offered comments on the piece, the two students discuss the piece. The consultant explains why he thinks specific instances should be revised.

The writer then either agrees or disagrees. If she agrees that revision is necessary, she may offer possibilities for how she would revise the material and seek the input of her partner. She would then go on to revise the material. If she disagrees, she should offer a reason.

Learning how to revise efficiently and effectively takes a long time and requires a major effort on your part and the parts of your students. These efforts are well worth the undertaking, because revision provides the opportunity to create quality material. It is through revision that your students will truly emerge as writers.

Reproducible Worksheets

Revising is a difficult activity for most students. The worksheets included in this section are designed to provide your students with practice in revision.

The worksheets, which include both articles and stories, cover a variety of topics. Students will find the worksheets challenging in that much of the material that should be revised is not technically wrong, but definitely could be improved. The exceptions are run-on sentences, fragments, unnecessary shifts in tense, faulty point of view, and errors in subject-verb agreement. You should mention to your students that punctuation and capitalization are correct on these worksheets. (Mechanics are addressed in Part 4, Proofreading.)

The reproducible Guidelines for Revision (page 154) offers students direction for revising their writing. You may find it helpful to distribute copies of the guidelines to your students or to create a poster of the guidelines and display it in your classroom.

Depending on the abilities of your students, you may find it beneficial to work together as a class and revise a few of the worksheets. Such practice can provide students with an excellent model of the revision process. Select examples that you feel would be most helpful to your students. Read through the piece and ask your students for suggestions for revision. Discuss their suggestions. It is probable that students will suggest different ways to revise the same material. Explain that most articles and stories can be revised in various manners, depending on the material and the purpose and outlook of the writer.

The worksheets proceed from relatively basic to more challenging. The directions for Worksheets 3.1 through 3.13 focus the attention of your students on specific elements to revise, while Worksheets 3.14 through 3.25 simply instruct students to revise the material and do not provide any hints of what weaknesses to look for. Each worksheet has several items that could be revised.

Before assigning any worksheet, review it to make sure it is appropriate for your students. If necessary, review the instructions and briefly discuss the topic to make sure students understand the material. The focus of students should be on revision, not the material.

Because revised articles and stories will vary, you should accept any reasonable revisions. The Answer Key offers a possible revision of each worksheet. After your students have finished their revisions, discuss the revised piece with the class. When students see other ways writing can be revised, their overall understanding of the revision process is enhanced.

Encourage your students to use their developing revision skills in their writing. It is through revision that they will achieve their best writing.

Guidelines for Revision

> Asking yourself the following questions can help you revise your writing.

1. Is my topic focused?

2. Do all of my ideas and details relate to my topic?

3. Does my writing have an opening, body, and closing?

4. Have I used paragraphs?

5. Does each paragraph have a main idea? Have I supported each main idea with details?

6. Have I used correct order and sequence?

7. Have I varied my sentence construction?

8. Have I used active constructions?

9. Have I used strong verbs?

10. Do my subjects and verbs agree?

11. Did I show and not tell?

12. Are my tenses consistent?

13. Is my point of view consistent?

14. Have I deleted all unnecessary information and words?

15. Have I expressed my ideas clearly?

3.1 The Moon

The moon is the Earth's natural satellite. About 240,000 miles away, it is our closest neighbor in space. Many people look at the moon each night. It is the only body in the solar system people have visited. The moon is barren. The moon is lifeless. The moon is a dangerous world. It has no atmosphere. It has no liquid water. The surface is covered with dust and craters. Scientists believe the craters were caused by meteorites crashing into the moon millions of years ago. Other planets have moons, too. In the shade, the temperature on the moon can be as cold as −280° Fahrenheit. In sunlight, the temperature can be as hot as 260° Fahrenheit. Scientists have learned much about the moon. They continue to study the moon. They hope that by learning more about the moon they will learn more about our solar system.

Revision

3.2 Geysers

A geyser is a natural hot spring. It shoots water and steam high into the air. Most geysers are found in three parts of the world. These three parts of the world are the western United States, Iceland, and New Zealand. Geysers occur when hot volcanic rock heats underground water to high temperatures. The water is heated. It begins to boil. It is becoming hotter and hotter. Steam forms and forces the water upward through cracks in the rock. There is enough pressure sometimes to shoot the hot water and steam into the air. The most famous geyser in the world is Old Faithful in Yellowstone National Park. This geyser, Old Faithful, erupts on average once every ninety-four minutes each day. Between 3,700 and 8,400 gallons of hot water shoot up to 170 feet in the air. Watching a geyser is exciting. It is very thrilling. Geysers are one of nature's thrilling shows.

Revision

3.3 The Beginnings of Roller Coasters

Directions: Revise the article. Make any changes you feel will improve it. Be sure it has an opening, body, and closing. (The revised article should have four paragraphs.) Eliminate any unnecessary information. Rewrite the revised article on a separate sheet of paper.

Modern roller coasters have their beginnings with Russian ice slides. Millions of people love roller coasters. The slides were first built in the mid-1600s. The ice slides were big structures. Some were between seventy and eighty feet high. During winter the slides were enjoyed by a lot of people. They were built of wood. They were covered with thick ice. Large sleds sped down the slide along an icy path for hundreds of feet. The builders even constructed stairs for riders to walk up the slides. Some historians believe the Russians also built the first true roller coaster in the late 1700s. It was a carriage with wheels. It was built in St. Petersburg. From these simple beginnings, we have the super roller coasters of today. A person can only imagine what future coasters will be like.

Revision

3.4 Healthy Teeth

Directions: Revise the article. Make any changes you feel will improve it. Especially pay attention to order and sequence. Eliminate any unnecessary information or words. Rewrite the article on a separate sheet of paper.

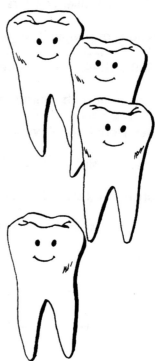

Having healthy teeth is important. Strong, healthy teeth help you to chew your food properly. Healthy teeth, they help you to speak clearly. Healthy teeth help you to look your best. It is very important to have healthy teeth.

To keep your teeth healthy, you must keep them clean. This is very, very important. Brush your teeth at least twice each day. You should brush them after breakfast and before bed. You should visit your dentist twice each year. The dentist will check for cavities and clean your teeth. Brush for at least three minutes. Be sure to brush in the back and along the sides of your teeth. You should clean your teeth with dental floss. The floss, which you should use every day, will clean places your toothbrush cannot reach.

Strong, clean teeth will help to keep you healthy. They, your strong, clean teeth, are something to smile about.

3.5 The Importance of Exercise

Directions: Revise the article. Make any changes you feel will improve it. Especially pay attention to subject-verb agreement and varying sentence structure. Rewrite the revised article on a separate sheet of paper.

Exercising each day will help to keep you in good health. It will also help you think better. It will help you sleep better. It will help you feel better.

Exercise help your body stay fit. It causes you to breathe more deeply. It makes your heart pump more strongly. It makes your muscles work harder. It makes your body use more calories. It helps to keep your body at a healthy weight.

You can exercise in many ways. You can walk. You can run. You can jog. You can play sports. You can ride your bike. You can skate. You can swim. You can dance. Any activity that make your heart beat faster is good.

Exercise is important for your health. You should try to exercise every day.

Revision

3.6 The Wandering Albatross

Directions: Revise the article. Make any changes you feel will improve it. Especially pay attention to unity, sentence structure, and subject-verb agreement. Eliminate any unnecessary information. Rewrite the revised article on a separate sheet of paper.

The wandering albatross is a large seabird. When it spreads it wings. The wings measure up to twelve feet from tip to tip. This is the largest wingspread of any living bird.

There are many kinds of albatrosses. Along with the wandering albatross. There is the black-footed albatross, the royal albatross, and the sooty albatross. There are even more. The wandering albatross is found over the oceans of the Southern Hemisphere.

Wandering albatrosses does not have a permanent home. They spend most of their lives flying over the oceans of the Southern Hemisphere. They feed on small fish. They can sleep on the sea's surface. When they become tired of flying. Like most seabirds, they drink seawater. They land only to mate, they make their nests on empty islands.

Because of its size, the wandering albatross have few predators. Most wandering albatrosses have long lives. The wandering albatross is thought to be one of the few birds to die of old age.

Revision

3.7 Doomed City

Directions: Revise the article. Make any changes you feel will improve it. Especially pay attention to unity, order, and sentence structure. Eliminate any unnecessary information. Rewrite the revised article on a separate sheet of paper.

Pompeii was a city in ancient Italy. It was built a few miles south of Mt. Vesuvius. Mt. Vesuvius is an active volcano. Pompeii was a wealthy city. Pompeii was always busy with trade.

The day of August 24 in the year A.D. 79 began like any other. Without warning. The top of Vesuvius exploded. Great clouds of smoke and ash rose high into the sky. Soon the light of the sun was blocked. The sky became dark.

People awoke that day and began their chores. In the distance the volcano sent lazy dark smoke into the sky. But this was normal. No one was worried.

Scientists study volcanoes. They hope to learn how to predict when a volcano will erupt.

The eruption continued throughout the day and night. The city was covered with ash and molten rock, it is estimated that two thousand people died. The doomed city of Pompeii disappeared in a day.

Revision

3.8 The Oregon Trail

The Oregon Trail was the most important pioneer route to the American Northwest. The trail was about two thousand miles long. It started in Independence, Missouri, it ended at the Columbia River in Oregon.

The journey over the trail was long. It was hard. It was dangerous, too. The trip could take as long as six months. Many hardships were faced by the pioneers. Terrible storms, illness, lack of food, and attacks by Native Americans were constant threats. Sometimes as many as half of the people of a wagon train died on the trail.

Despite the hardships. The trail was followed by thousands of pioneers. They believed that the Oregon Trail was a way to a new life.

3.9 Laura Ingalls Wilder

Directions: Revise the article. Make any changes you feel will improve it. Especially pay attention to sentence structure and active constructions. Rewrite the revised article on a separate sheet of paper.

Laura Ingalls was born in Pepin, Wisconsin, on February 7, 1867. Laura Ingalls was the second daughter of Charles and Caroline Ingalls.

During her childhood, Laura traveled westward with her family in a covered wagon. Wisconsin, Kansas, and Minnesota were crossed by the Ingalls family, the Dakota Territory was where they finally settled.

Laura loved living on the prairie. Life could be hard. It was full of joy. Laura enjoyed helping her parents with the chores.

Laura grew up. She married Almanzo Wilder. Laura and Almanzo moved to Mansfield, Missouri. A home there was built by Laura and Almanzo.

Her family's pioneer days were remembered fondly by Laura. She would tell stories about living on the prairie to Rose, her daughter. Rose, her daughter, suggested that her mother write the stories down so that others could read them. These stories became the Little House series.

Revision

3.10 Moving In

Directions: Revise the story. Make any changes you feel will improve it. Especially pay attention to varying sentence structure and verb tenses. Rewrite the revised story on a separate sheet of paper.

Rachel stood in her new room. Boxes are everywhere. The room was bigger than her room in her old house. The room in her old house was small. The new room did not feel like home.

Rachel missed her old house. She missed her old friends. She is worried about making new friends.

Rachel unpacked a few boxes. She went outside. She sat on the front steps. She looked around the yard. There were flowers and trees. The yard was pretty.

Rachel noticed a girl from the house across the street walking toward her. The girl is about Rachel's age.

"Hi, I'm Danielle," the girl says. "But my friends call me Dani. . . ."

Revision

3.11 The Messy Room

Directions: Revise the story. Make any changes you feel will improve it. Especially pay attention to varying sentence structure, strong verbs, and descriptions. Rewrite the revised story on a separate sheet of paper.

Jason was in his room. It was messy. He was upset.

He could not find his science report. He had finished it yesterday. He finished it right after school. Then he had gone out to play with his friends.

He looked at his messy desk. His mother was always urging him to be neater. He went through the stuff on it. He went through the drawers in the desk. They were messy, too. He searched his messy dresser. He searched under his messy bed.

He tried to remember where he put the report. Suddenly he remembered.

He picked up his knapsack. It was in a folder. He had put it in the knapsack yesterday so that he would not lose it.

Jason heard the school bus. He picked up his knapsack. He went to the door.

Revision

3.12 The Monster Coaster

Directions: Revise the story. Make any changes you feel will improve it. Especially pay attention to varying sentence structure, point of view, and verb tenses. Rewrite the revised story on a separate sheet of paper.

Maria stood in front of the big roller coaster. Carlos, her younger brother was with her.

It was called the Monster. Maria had been looking forward to riding it for weeks. But now she is not sure she wants to.

It was so high. It was so fast. And it had three loops. Maria likes fast rides, but this one scares her.

"Come on, Maria," says Carlos. "Let's get in line." He takes my hand and started pulling me.

At first Maria does not move. It was as if my feet will not go.

"Maria, come on," said Carlos. "You're not afraid, are you?"

Maria smiled weakly. If her little brother was not afraid, I should not be afraid either.

"Let's go," Maria says. She led Carlos to the line.

Revision

3.13 The Game

Directions: Revise the story. Make any changes you feel will improve it. Especially pay attention to point of view and descriptions. Rewrite the revised story on a separate sheet of paper.

One second was left in the championship game between the Hawks and Cougars. The score was 38 to 38.

Kevin Williams, the Cougars' youngest player, was at the foul line. If he made either of his two foul shots, the Cougars would be champions. But Kevin was not a good foul shooter.

The referee gave him the ball.

I took a deep breath. I bounced the ball to calm myself.

I looked up at the basket. I aimed and let it go. It missed. The home crowd sounded sad.

The referee handed Kevin the ball again. Once more I bounced the ball to steady myself. I aimed and let it go.

I watched it go through the net.

Revision

3.14 The Sun

The sun is a star. Like other stars, it is a giant ball of burning gases. It is made up mostly of hydrogen. This is a gas. The sun is about 93 million miles from Earth. This is very, very far. Earth is one of the nine planets that orbit the sun. Inside the sun, hydrogen atoms are fused (forced together) to make helium. Great amounts of energy are produced. Some of this energy reaches the Earth. As light and heat. The temperature on the surface of the sun is about 11,000° Fahrenheit. Inside the sun, near the center, the temperature is about 35 million degrees Fahrenheit. The sun makes life possible on the Earth. Without the sun, the Earth would be a cold, dark planet. It would be lifeless.

3.15 The Bear Facts

Bears are large mammals. There are several kinds of bears. Black bears were once found throughout North America. Now they are found mostly in wilderness areas. Black bears are one of the smallest bears, they weigh between two hundred and four hundred pounds. Grizzly bears are among the most dangerous bears. They can weigh up to one thousand pounds. Other animals are hunted by grizzlies for food. Grizzlies may be brown, black, or cream-colored. The fur on their shoulders and backs is often tipped with white. This gives them a "grizzled" look. Polar bears are found on the islands of the Arctic Ocean. They are big bears. Polar bears may be ten feet tall and weigh up to fifteen hundred pounds. Seals, young walruses, and fish are hunted by polar bears. Their thick white coats keep them warm in icy temperatures. Bears are found in many parts of the world. Bears are among nature's most interesting animals.

Revision

3.16 Smokey Bear

Directions: Revise the article. Make any changes you feel will improve it. Rewrite the revised article on a separate sheet of paper.

Many people have heard of Smokey Bear. They know Smokey is a symbol for fire prevention. Not everyone knows the story of the real Smokey.

On a spring day in 1950, parts of New Mexico were burned by a terrible fire. A baby black bear was found in a tree by firefighters. The men gently took the cub from the tree, they did not know what to do with him. A rancher who had been helping the firefighters offered to take the injured cub home. The cub had climbed the tree to try to escape the flames. But his paws and back were burned.

A forest ranger heard about the cub. He drove to the ranch. Had the injured cub flown to Santa Fe. His injuries were treated by a veterinarian there.

Eventually the cub was sent to Washington, D.C. He was given a home in the National Zoo. The cub became known as Smokey Bear.

Revision

3.17 Johnny Appleseed

Directions: Revise the article. Make any changes you feel will improve it. Rewrite the revised article on a separate sheet of paper.

Johnny Appleseed was a real man. His name was John Chapman, he was born in 1774 in Leominster, Massachusetts.

Settlers moved westward. John went with them. For nearly fifty years. John planted apple trees. He planted apple trees in what became the states of Ohio, Michigan, Illinois, and Indiana. People called John the Apple Tree Man or Johnny Appleseed.

John worked alone. He walked across the wilderness. He would find a good spot for planting. He would clear the land. He would plant apple seeds. He would build a brush fence around the spot to keep animals out. An orchard would fill the spot.

John Chapman died in 1845. The apple orchards he left behind were a gift to the settlers who came after him.

Revision

3.18 The Ice

With very, very nervous fingers Tamara tightened the laces of her ice skates. She took a deep breath.

"Don't worry," her coach said. "You'll do fine."

That made Tamara worry even more. That was what people told her last winter. Tamara remembered. Trying to jump and turn in the air for the first time. The awful, terrible pain of her ankle breaking would never be forgotten by Tamara. Her ankle hurt really, really badly for days. Her slow recovery took months.

Tamara started skating again a few weeks ago. She had not tried to jump and spin, she would today.

Tamara stood and stepped onto the ice, her heart was thumping.

"Good luck," was said by her coach.

Tamara nodded.

She skated around the rink. She tried to build up her courage.

She began to skate faster and faster. She lifted off the ice. She rose and spun.

She landed perfectly!

3.19 Giant Squid

Directions: Revise the article. Make any changes you feel will improve it. Rewrite the revised article on a separate sheet of paper.

When ancient sailors reported seeing sea monsters. They might have seen a giant squid. The giant squid is a frightening animal. It is a scary animal, too.

The name *giant squid* fits this creature. The giant squid can grow to be 150 feet long. The giant squid's big eyes can be 3 feet across. The giant squid has long tentacles. The giant squid's prey is caught with its tentacles.

The giant squid is one of the fastest creatures in the ocean. It can draw water into its body. It can then force the water out. That shoots the animal forward like a rocket.

Giant squid live deep in the ocean. They live far below the surface of the ocean. Sometimes they come to the surface. This creature could have been mistaken for a sea monster by ancient sailors.

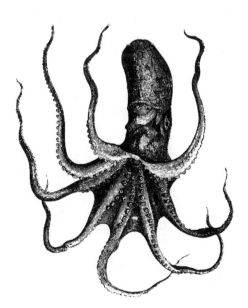

Revision

3.20 The Earl of Sandwich

Directions: Revise the article. Make any changes you feel will improve it. Rewrite the revised article on a separate sheet of paper.

John Montagu is a nobleman. He lived in England in the 1700s. He is the fourth Earl of Sandwich. He was also a well-known gambler.

When he was gambling. He would sit at the table for hours. One day he is gambling. He gets hungry. But he did not want to leave the game. So he sends a servant to bring him meat between two slices of bread.

Other gamblers think this is a good idea. They got hungry. They said something like, "I'll have what Sandwich had." Soon the name Sandwich came to mean meat between two slices of bread.

The sandwich was named after the Earl of Sandwich in 1762. Since then countless sandwiches have been made.

3.21 Little Dinosaurs

Directions: Revise the article. Make any changes you feel will improve it. Rewrite the revised article on a separate sheet of paper.

When most people think of dinosaurs. They think of big creatures. But there are little dinosaurs too.

The smallest dinosaur is thought to be a microraptor. This dinosaur was about sixteen inches long. This dinosaur was about the size of a crow.

Saltopus was a little bigger. Than a microraptor. It was about two feet long. It was the size of a small cat. It walks on two legs. It has a long head. It has dozens of sharp teeth.

Compsognathus was about the size of a big chicken. It was about three feet long. It has two thin legs. It has three-toed feet. It had a long tail. It had a pointed head, had sharp teeth.

Even smaller dinosaurs may be discovered by scientists someday. But most people will probably continue to think of dinosaurs as big creatures.

Revision

3.22 An Early Flyer

Directions: Revise the article. Make any changes you feel will improve it. Rewrite the revised article on a separate sheet of paper.

Wiley Post was born in Grand Plain, Texas, in 1899. He did not have much formal schooling. He became one of the most famous early pilots.

In 1931, Post and his navigator flew around the world. His navigator was Harold Charles Gatty. They made the flight in eight days, fifteen hours, and fifty-one minutes. A world record was set by them.

Two years later, in 1933, it was decided by Post to fly around the world by himself. He set a new record of seven days, eighteen hours, and forty-nine minutes.

Wiley Post died on August 15, 1935. His plane crashed at Point Barrow, Alaska. He was called a national hero.

3.23 A Busy Day

Directions: Revise the story. Make any changes you feel will improve it. Rewrite the revised story on a separate sheet of paper.

Kareem woke up early on Saturday. He had a busy day planned.

After breakfast, Kareem went to soccer practice. He was the goalie for his team, he liked soccer.

After lunch, Kareem helped his father in the yard. They raked leaves. They trimmed the hedges. His father mowed the lawn. Kareem weeded the flower beds. They worked in the yard all afternoon.

In the evening, Kareem's friends came. His friends' names were David and Charles. The boys decided to watch a movie. After the movie was done, his friends went home. Kareem watched TV a little while with his parents.

He soon went to bed. It had been a busy day. He was tired

Revision

3.24 Platypus

The platypus is a very strange, unusual animal. It is a mammal. It also has traits of a duck. Another name for this very strange, unusual animal is the duckbill.

Platypuses are found in Australia. They live in burrows along the banks of rivers. They make their homes near water.

An adult platypus is about fourteen inches in length. It has a long body. It has a flat tail. It uses its flat tail for swimming.

The platypus have many traits of mammals. It is warm-blooded, it has fur, it feeds its young milk.

But the platypus also have some traits of ducks. Instead of a nose and mouth. The platypus has a leathery bill. It has webbed feet for swimming. Like a duck, it lays eggs. A baby platypus hatches from an egg.

The platypus is truly a very strange, unusual animal.

3.25 The Myth of Daedalus and Icarus

Directions: Revise the story. Make any changes you feel will improve it. Rewrite the revised story on a separate sheet of paper.

Daedalus and his son Icarus were imprisoned on the island of Crete. In hopes of escaping. A very dangerous and very daring plan was thought of by Daedalus. He would build wings of wax and feathers. For Icarus and himself.

Daedalus begins his work. When the day came that the wings were done, he calls to Icarus. He warns Icarus not to fly too close to the sun. The heat would melt the wax. The wings would fall apart.

Icarus promises his father he would be careful. But once they set off. The boy is overcome with the thrill of flying like a bird.

Daedalus sees his son flying higher and higher. He called to him that he was too close to the sun. Yet the boy keeps going higher.

Soon the wax on Icarus's wings begins to melt. Feathers started to fall off. The boy flapped the wings wildly. But the wings came apart, he fell into the sea and drowned.

Revision

PART 4

Proofreading

Proofreading is the part of the writing process that puts the final polish on a piece. Proofreading should not be done until writing has been revised. It is a time for authors to catch and correct any remaining errors in punctuation, capitalization, spelling, and word usage that were missed during revision. Proofreading is the final preparation before a piece is shared with an audience.

Some authors, especially young or inexperienced writers, mistakenly believe that proofreading is the easiest stage of the writing process. Because revision has been completed, they feel that the writing is done. Proofreading, however, is just as demanding as the other stages of writing. While it is true that most errors have been corrected by this time, the errors that remain often are subtle ones; by now the author may have become so close to the piece that mistakes are hard to find. Moreover, the author is anxious to finish the piece, and he may proofread in haste or without the necessary attentiveness. If an author has done a thorough job of revision, proofreading is much like looking for that needle in the haystack.

For just about every piece, no matter how diligent the writer was during revision, a few mistakes remain. Proofreading requires concentration and a good eye.

Proofreading Strategies

Proofreading is different from ordinary reading. Ordinary reading includes a significant amount of skimming. The average reader focuses on only a few words per line and skims the rest. This is usually enough for the reader to gain an understanding of the material. Proofreading, though, requires that the proofreader read and examine every word and punctuation mark.

When done properly, proofreading is slow, tedious work. Anything less is likely to be inadequate.

Explain to your students that every writer must proofread her work to correct any remaining mistakes before she can say it is finished. Proofreading is the last step before sharing writing with readers. Write these general guidelines on an overhead projector or the board, and discuss them with your students:

1. Read slowly and concentrate on punctuation, capitalization, spelling, and word usage.
2. Look at the page to make sure paragraphs are fully indented, margins are correct, and there are no gaps in spacing.
3. Proofread the piece two or three times. It is likely that each time a few more minor errors will be found. Only when no more errors are found is proofreading done.

Instruct your students to select an example of their work to proofread. This might be a previously completed piece or a piece that they have just finished. Have them proofread the piece with care and concentration.

Encourage your students to follow these suggestions whenever proofreading their work. With practice and experience, every writer eventually develops his own methods for proofreading.

Proofreading and Computer Screens

Without doubt, computers have made the work of most writers easier. The capabilities of the machines for composing and revising are without question. Proofreading on a computer screen, however, poses problems for many writers.

Reading text on a computer screen can be trying to the eyes. Consequently, some writers tend to read material with less deliberation than they use with text printed on paper. In addition, text on paper has a different "look" from text on a screen, despite a print preview. When an author reads text on paper, he is more apt to concentrate and examine words and punctuation with greater care.

Of course, some writers do quite well proofing on a computer screen. I suspect that many of the current generation of students will eventually fall into this category. Growing up with computers and playing countless video games will provide them with a high level of comfort in writing, revising, and proofreading written material on a computer screen.

Because it is likely that many of your students will do at least some of their proofreading on a computer, you should provide these guidelines on an overhead projector or the board:

1. Read slowly and carefully. [Explain that most people tend to read faster on a computer screen than a printed page.]
2. Use the cursor arrow to go through the text one line at a time.
3. Read every word of each line before going to the next line.
4. Concentrate on every piece of punctuation.
5. Use the print preview to check the page for paragraphs, skipped spaces, and unnecessary returns.

After discussing the guidelines, encourage students to proofread a finished piece on a computer screen. Suggest to your students that if they are not comfortable proofing on a computer screen, they should print the material and proof the printed text.

The Value of Proofreading Partners

The work of just about every writer—whether student or professional—benefits from the attention of an editor. Obviously, the more skilled an editor is the greater the benefits, but in most cases even student editors can help a classmate during proofreading. Because students often have trouble stepping back from their writing to view it objectively, proofreading can be difficult for them. The author may pass over small, subtle errors that others quickly recognize. A proofreading partner can help find many of the minor errors that the writer may overlook.

Proofreading partners should be students who work well together. In some cases, good friends may turn out to be ideal partners who help each other, but in other cases friends may find it hard to concentrate on work when they are together. You should match students who will complement each other during proofreading.

I encourage students to have a dictionary and grammar book handy when they are proofreading. An author's stylebook is also helpful. During proofreading students should underline any errors they find in their partner's work. An alternative to marking clean pages is to use stick-on notes. If partners cannot agree whether an item is wrong, they should consult an appropriate reference book. They should check with you only after consulting references.

Organize your students into proofreading pairs. If you have an odd number of students in class, you may allow a team of three. Explain that partners are to proofread each other's writing and identify any remaining errors in punctuation, capitalization, spelling, or word usage. Instruct your students to underline any mistakes they find in pencil, or use stick-on notes. After proofreading, the proofreader consults with the author and notes the mistakes she found. If the author disagrees with any of the supposed mistakes, the students check a reference source. The author then corrects any mistakes and proceeds to produce the final copy. I encourage every student to proofread the final copy once more. The students then switch roles; the previous author becomes the proofreader for her partner's work.

Proofreading is not a task of writing to be taken lightly. It is the final preparation of a piece for its audience.

Reproducible Worksheets

Proofreading is a challenging task for most students. The worksheets in this section are designed to provide your students with practice in proofreading.

The worksheets, which include both articles and stories, cover a variety of topics. Errors are concentrated in punctuation, capitalization, and word usage.

The reproducible Guidelines for Proofreading (page 186) offers students direction in their proofreading efforts. You may find it helpful to distribute copies of the guidelines to your students or to create a poster of the guidelines and display it in your classroom.

Depending on the abilities of your students, you may decide to work together as a class and proofread a few of the worksheets. The practice can help students to recognize the types of errors they should look for during proofreading. Choose examples that you feel would be most beneficial. Read through the piece as a class and ask your students to identify the errors. Correct the worksheet together.

The worksheets in this part proceed from relatively basic—for example, focusing on end punctuation, commas, and capitalization—to more challenging. Along with general errors in punctuation and capitalization, the directions for Worksheets 4.1 through 4.15 focus the attention of students on specific errors. The worksheets average about ten errors each, some a few less and some a few more. Many of the errors are obvious; some are tricky and require sharp concentration.

Before assigning a worksheet, I suggest that you review it to make sure it is appropriate for your students. If necessary, go over the instructions and briefly discuss the topic to make sure that students understand the material. When proofreading, students should not be hampered by unfamiliar or difficult material.

The Answer Key for the worksheets is found on page 213. Note: While most of the corrections are clear-cut, a few, especially concerning the use of commas, are open to interpretation of the context. Accept reasonable corrections in such cases.

After your students have proofread and corrected a worksheet, you should go over the worksheet with the class. This enables students to see any errors that they might have failed to correct.

As students gain experience with proofreading, their proofreading skills will grow. Proofreading will help them to present polished writing to their readers.

Guidelines for Proofreading

Use the following guidelines when proofreading your writing.

1. Sentences begin with capital letters.

2. Sentences end with correct punctuation.

3. Paragraphs are indented.

4. Proper nouns and proper adjectives are capitalized.

5. Commas are used correctly (between the items in a list, to connect compound sentences, and after introductory words, phrases, and clauses).

6. Apostrophes are used correctly (with possessive nouns and contractions).

7. Pronouns are used correctly.

8. Quotation marks are used correctly (for dialogue and for the titles of short stories, articles, poems, and songs).

9. Italics and underlining are used correctly (for the titles of books, the names of newspapers and magazines, and the titles of movies).

10. Words are used correctly (especially homophones such as *there, their,* and *they're; your* and *you're; its* and *it's;* and *to, too,* and *two*).

Proofreading

4.1 The Gila Monster

Directions: Proofread and correct the article. Pay close attention to errors in ending punctuation, commas, and capitalization. Make your corrections on this sheet.

The Gila monster is not a monster. It is a lizard. It is the largest lizard in the United States. it is also the only poisonous lizard in our Country

The Gila monster is found in the Desert areas of Arizona Nevada, Utah, and new Mexico. It is named after the Gila river.

An adult Gila monster is easy to recognize. It is about two feet long and weighs between three and five pounds. It has a thick body, and short legs. Its black, scaly body is covered with orange pink and yellow spots.

The poison of a Gila monster is usually not strong enough to kill Humans. But the bite of the lizard, is painful.

Proofreading

4.2 How to Study for Tests

Directions: Proofread and correct the article. Pay close attention to errors in ending punctuation, commas, and capitalization. Make your corrections on this sheet.

Do you know how to study for tests. Here are some suggestions.

On the days leading up to the Test, listen to any reviews your teacher gives. This will help you find out what may be on the Test. You will be able to study the right material. If you have any questions about the material, ask your teacher?

Begin studying a day or two before the Test go over your notes and key parts of your textbook. Do not wait until the last minute, to study. Students who study ahead of time usually do better than those who cram.

On the day of the Test be confident. people who study do better than people who do not study.

4.3 The Family Picnic

Directions: Proofread and correct the story. Pay close attention to errors in ending punctuation, commas, and capitalization. Make your corrections on this sheet.

Katie woke up early on saturday! She was too excited to sleep! Today was the day of her family's picnic.

Each year the Morgan Family met at Ellis park for a picnic. All of Katie's aunts uncles and cousins would be there.

After breakfast Katie helped her mother pack food in coolers. They packed, sandwiches, salads, and desserts.

The drive to the park seemed to take forever As they entered the park, Katie's father headed for lake Ellis where the Picnic Grounds were located. Nearing the lake, Katie saw that people were already there.

She smiled. This, would be a great day.

Proofreading

Name _____   Date _____

4.4 Frogs and Toads

> **Directions:** Proofread and correct the article. Pay close attention to errors in ending punctuation, commas, and capitalization. Make your corrections on this sheet.

Frogs and Toads are amphibians. They are animals that can live both in water and on land. Although frogs and toads are much alike they are different too. Do you know how they are different.

Frogs spend much of their lives in water. Their bodies are usually slimmer than the bodies of toads they have smooth skin and they have long legs for jumping.

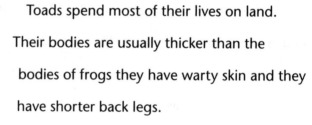

Toads spend most of their lives on land. Their bodies are usually thicker than the bodies of frogs they have warty skin and they have shorter back legs.

Of course for most People these are not very big differences. To them frogs and toads are more alike than different.

Proofreading

4.5 Why Plants and Animals Become Extinct

Directions: Proofread and correct the article. Pay close attention to errors in ending punctuation, commas, and capitalization. Make your corrections on this sheet.

Throughout history many plants and animals have become extinct. these plants and animals are no longer alive anywhere on our planet. Plants, and animals become extinct for many reasons.

Big changes in Climate can cause plants and animals to become extinct. If the climate of an area that once got much rain becomes very dry, some plants and animals may die out?

Sometimes people change the land where plants, and animals live For example, people cut down Forests. They may use wood to build houses or they may clear land for farming. The plants and animals that lived there may die.

Overhunting can cause animals to become extinct. Before the settlers came, buffalo ranged across the american Great Plains. By the end of the nineteenth century buffaloes were hunted almost to extinction.

Every effort should be made to protect plants and animals from extinction. Once a plant, or animal, becomes extinct it is too late.

Proofreading

4.6 The Test

Directions: Proofread and correct the story. Pay close attention to errors in punctuation and capitalization. Especially pay attention to the use of commas and apostrophes. Make your corrections on this sheet.

Marissa went down the hall toward her classroom. She felt foolish coming back to school. But she had forgotten her history book. without her history book, she wouldnt be able to study for the big history test Tomorrow.

History was a hard subject for Marissa. If she wanted a high grade on her report card she had to study.

Just before she got to the classroom she saw a paper on the floor. When she picked the paper up, her eyes widened. It was the tests answer key.

This was her chance to get a good grade. She held the key for a long moment.

That would be cheating and Marissa wasn't a cheater.

She went into her classroom. Her teacher ms. Carter was there. Marissa went to the desk and handed the key to ms. Carter.

4.7 Deserts

Directions: Proofread and correct the article. Pay close attention to errors in punctuation and capitalization. Especially pay attention to the use of commas and apostrophes. Make your corrections on this sheet.

With it's oceans lakes, and rivers, the Earth has plenty of water. But not all parts of the Earth have a lot of water. about one-fifth of the Earth's land is desert.

Desert's are dry areas of land. Some deserts get only an inch or two of rainfall every year.

Although it is hard for life to survive in deserts many plants and animals make the desert their home. Plants such as the Cactus live in deserts. Animals such as Snakes, Lizards, and Camels live in deserts too.

People also live in or near deserts. Many of these people believe that deserts have a special beauty. This beauty, is found nowhere else on our planet.

Proofreading

4.8 Earthquakes

Earthquakes are more common than most people think. Thousands of earthquakes occur each year but most are so weak they aren't felt. Only about one out of five hundred earthquakes causes damage

In the past, people didnt know what caused earthquakes? Today scientists' know that the Earth's crust, it's outer layer is divided into great pieces. These pieces called plates are made of Rock. The plates move slowly in different directions. They may move past each other away from each other or toward each other. Sometimes a long crack, called a fault, forms between plates. If enough stress builds up along a fault an earthquake occurs.

Minor earthquakes cause little damage. Major quakes can destroy buildings bridges and roads. They can cause thousands of deaths.

4.9 The Race

Directions: Proofread and correct the story. Pay close attention to errors in punctuation and capitalization. Especially pay attention to the use of commas, apostrophes, and quotation marks. Make your corrections on this sheet.

It was Field Day at Manuels School. As he waited for his turn to run Manuel was worried. He was the fastest boy in the fifth grade but that could change today.

Mr. Wilkins, Manuels teacher called the last four boys to the starting line.

Manuel stepped forward. This was a race against time. Whoever ran the fastest would be the fastest runner in the fifth grade?

Manuel took a deep breath, and bent his legs. Every muscle was ready. He looked at the finish line at the end of the field. Another teacher Ms Edwards was there with a stopwatch.

"On your mark! said Mr. Wilkins. Get set! Go!"

The boys began. Manuel took powerful strides. he heard kids cheering but his thoughts were only on running. He was pulling ahead.

Manuel crossed the line first.

Sixteen point three seconds ms. Edwards said!

Manuel smiled That was the best time of the day. He was still the fastest runner in the fifth grade.

Proofreading

4.10 A Business Letter

Directions: Proofread and correct the letter. Pay close attention to errors in punctuation and capitalization. Especially pay attention to the use of commas and colons. Make your corrections on this sheet.

123 Mountain road

High Point WA 00000

September 25 2006

Mr William Connors, Circulation Manager

Rugged Outdoors Magazine

50 Carter street

Centerville, CA 00000

Dear Mr. Connors,

I would like to subscribe to "Rugged Outdoors Magazine." Enclosed is a check for $19.95 for a subscription for one year.

Thank you.

Yours Truly.

Jon Petersen

Jon Petersen

4.11 Best Friends

Directions: Proofread and correct the article. Pay close attention to errors in punctuation and capitalization. Especially pay attention to the use of apostrophes and pronouns. Make your corrections on this sheet.

Me and Jimmy are best friends. We've been best friends since kindergarten. Some kids think its strange that a girl and a boy in fifth grade are best friends. But Jimmy and me have a lot in common.

We live next door to each other. We both like sports we like the same type of music, and we like the same kinds of Movies. But most important, we just like hanging out together. Jimmys easy to talk to and he's always willing to help when i have a problem. I do the same for him.

No matter what happens I know I can count on Jimmy. I suppose thats whats best about being best friends.

Proofreading

4.12 Arbor Day

Directions: Proofread and correct the article. Pay close attention to errors in punctuation and capitalization. Especially pay attention to the use of apostrophes, pronouns, and parentheses. Make your corrections on this sheet.

Arbor Day is a day for planting trees. All fifty States in the US. celebrate Arbor Day.

Julius Sterling Morton 1832–1902 founded the first Arbor Day in Nebraska on April 10 1872. Morton believed that Nebraskas Land could be improved by the planting of trees.

Nebraskas first Arbor Day was a great success! People planted more than one million trees. A second Arbor Day took place in 1884 and also was successful. In 1885, Nebraska made Arbor Day a holiday and set April 22nd to celebrate it. April 22nd was Julius Sterling Mortons birthday.

In the following years, other states set aside there own Arbor Days. Although the dates vary because of climate, Arbor Day remains a day for planting trees. It is a day people throughout the Country can celebrate our environment.

Proofreading

4.13 Play Ball!

Directions: Proofread and correct the story. Pay close attention to errors in punctuation and capitalization. Especially pay attention to quotation marks, apostrophes, and pronouns. Make your corrections on this sheet.

Jason looked at the darkening sky. He turned to Martin his friend.

"I bet its going to rain" Jason said.

"It'll hold off until after the game, said Martin."

The two boys had just arrived at the baseball field. Some of the players of both teams were already their. This was the first game of the season and all the boys were excited.

Coach Smith instructed the boys to begin warm-ups.

Jason and Martin took their places with there teammates and began stretching.

Jason looked back at the sky. He loved baseball and had been looking forward to this first game for weeks.

You worry too much," said Martin. From the looks of those clouds, it wont rain for a while."

"I hope you're right," said Jason.

A little while later the game was ready to start.

"Play Ball!" the umpire called.

"See," said Martin. "You worry too much."

Jason smiled. "Maybe your right."

Proofreading

4.14 Reading

Everybody in my family likes to read. Books, magazines, and newspapers are everywhere in our home.

My father reads the newspaper every morning. He reads the "New York Times" on the train to work. He also reads magazines. His favorite is *Newsweek*.

My mother likes to read novels. She reads a new novel every week. She likes Mysteries the best.

Stephie my sister likes short stories and poems. One of her favorite short stories is *The Open Window* by H. H. Munro. Her favorite poem is Robert Frost's "The Road Not Taken."

I like to read novels. My favorites are science fiction. If I had to pick one favorite, I would choose "A wrinkle in Time" by Madeleine L' Engle.

4.15 The Big Slope

Directions: Proofread and correct the story. Pay close attention to errors in punctuation and capitalization. Especially pay attention to the use of quotation marks, apostrophes, and word usage. Make your corrections on this sheet.

Kyra stood on the top of the Mountain. She looked down the ski slope. Breakneck Trail disappeared in the distance. She took a deep breath too steady herself.

"Dont be afraid," said Mia her big sister. "You can make it down."

"Im not worried about making it down, said Kyra. She forced a smile. "I'm worried about how many pieces I'll be in."

Mia patted her on the shoulder. "You don't have to do this, she said."

"Yes, I do" said Kyra. "This is the only trail on this mountain Ive never gone down."

Mia smiled. "Keep you're knees bent, she said, and remember to lean into the turns."

"Wish me luck," Kyra said. She pushed off with her poles and started down the trail.

As she picked up speed she heard Mias voice behind her.

"Good luck."

Proofreading

4.16 Sound

What causes sound. The sounds of a crying baby, the slamming of a door or the roar of a jets engines are all produced in the same way.

Sound is caused by vibrations. When something vibrates it moves back and forth rapidly. Imagine pulling a string on a Guitar. As the string vibrates, it makes a sound.

Vibrating objects cause the molecules in the air around them to move. As the molecules move the vibrations travel, through the air in waves. When these waves reach your ear, you hair the sound.

As sound waves move away from a vibrating object they become weaker. A sound becomes fainter the farther away you are from its source.

4.17 Checkers

Directions: Proofread and correct the article. Pay close attention to errors in punctuation, capitalization, and word usage. Make your corrections on this sheet.

Have you ever played checkers? If you have you have played one of the Worlds oldest games.

Games similar to checkers were played by the ancient egyptians about thirty-five hundred years ago. A form of the game was also played in ancient Greece. the modern form of checkers appeared about five hundred years ago.

Checkers is a game of skill. Two players' play against each other. Each player has twelve playing pieces on a board that has sixty-four squares. the goal of the game is to capture an opponents pieces. The best players' think ahead and take advantage of there opponent's mistakes.

Checkers is played around the world. Minor rules vary somewhat from country to country but the basic game is the same.

4.18 Safety First

Directions: Proofread and correct the article. Pay close attention to errors in punctuation, capitalization, and word usage. Make your corrections on this sheet.

Most accidents happen at home. Although nobody can prevent every accident you can prevent many accidents by being careful and using common sense.

Many accidents occur in the kitchen. always be careful around a stove so that you don't get burned. Don't leave paper towels napkins, or cloths near the stove. Handle knives with care. Dont touch their sharp blades and always cut away from your body. Keep knives in a safe place wear young children cant get them.

Many accidents also occur in the bathroom. Never use electrical Appliances such as a hear dryer near water. Use a rubber mat to prevent anyone from slipping in the bathtub. keeping soap in a soap dish will help prevent people from slipping on it.

Accidents can happen to anyone: But using common sense and being careful can reduce the chances of an accident happening to you.

4.19 Whale-Watching

Hallie took her seat in the boat. She was not pleased. Her parents and her were spending one of there vacation days looking for whales. her mom called it whale-watching. Hallie would have liked to spend the day at the lake, where her parents had rented a cabin for the weak.

"This will be exciting Hallies mother said.

"I'd rather be swimming at the lake Hallie said."

"You can swim every day for the rest of the week said her father. "But you can't see a whale every day."

Hallie didnt understand what could be so great about seeing a whale. She pulled up the hood of her Sweatshirt to block the cool breeze.

It was early afternoon when one of the boats crewmen pointed ahead.

"There! he cried.

Hallie turned and saw a fantastic creature rise from the water.

"Its beautiful," she said, and she forgot all about swimming.

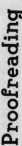

Proofreading

205

4.20 Colors

Colors make the world a brighter place. Imagine how dull the World would be without colors?

Colors can be divided into three kinds primary, secondary, and intermediate.

The primary colors are red yellow and blue. These are known as the basic colors. They cant be made bye mixing any other colors.

The secondary colors are orange green, and violet. Secondary colors are made by mixing to primary colors. Mixing red and yellow makes orange. Mixing yellow and blue makes green. Mixing blue and red makes violet.

Intermediate colors are made by mixing primary and secondary colors. Mixing white, or black with colors will make them lighter or darker.

It is remarkable that all colors are based on combinations of red, yellow, and blue. What a colorful world, the Earth is!

4.21 Sasha, Come Down

Directions: Proofread and correct the story. Pay close attention to errors in punctuation, capitalization, and word usage. Make your corrections on this sheet.

I was doing my homework when Annie my little sister came running into my room.

"Cassie come quick!" she cried.

"What's wrong," I said.

"Its Sasha! Annie said between sobs. She's stuck in a big tree." Sasha was our cat.

I followed her downstairs and out the front door.

I looked up at the big oak tree in our yard. Sure enough Sasha was sitting on a high branch. Although she had climbed up she was afraid to climb down.

"Sasha, come down," I said. But all I received was a sad meow.

Their wasn't anything I could do except to keep calling Sasha to come down. But the cat wouldnt budge.

Fortunately, my father and mother soon came home from work. My father got the Ladder from the Garage and got Sasha.

I smiled as annie scolded the silly cat.

"Sasha don't ever do that again," she said.

Proofreading

4.22 Rainbows

When sunlight strikes water droplets in the air a rainbow may form. The rainbow makes an arc in the sky. Sometimes its ends seem to touch the Earth.

Why does a rainbow appear when sunlight hits water droplets. The answer lies in sunlight. a ray of sunlight contains all the colors of the spectrum, red, orange, yellow, green, blue, and violet. Tiny water droplets separate the sunlight into it's different colors. Under the right conditions that creates a rainbow.

Rainbows most often are seen near the end of a rain shower. But they can also be seen in the spray of a waterfall a fountain or a garden hose.

According two Legend a pot of gold is at the end of a rainbow. Of course no one can ever reach the end of a rainbow. As you approach a rainbow, it seems to move farther a way and soon disappears.

4.23 Babysitting

Directions: Proofread and correct the story. Pay close attention to errors in punctuation, capitalization, and word usage. Make your corrections on this sheet.

Lateesha rang the doorbell to the home of Mr. and Mrs Morgan. This was the first time she was to babysit for there son Nathan. She hoped Nathan, who was only five years old would behave. Her friend Christina had babysat for Nathan once, and she would never do it again.

Mrs. Morgan opened the door with a big smile.

Lateesha saw Nathan standing in the living room. He was smiling to. He seemed like a nice boy.

After Mrs. Morgan gave Lateesha instructions, her and her husband got ready to leave.

"Remember Lateesha," mrs. Morgan said at the door, Nathan must be in bed by nine."

"I won't forget." Lateesha said.

For the next two hours she read to Nathan, they colored, and they watched TV. Nathan was so delightful that Lateesha began to wonder if Christina had babysat four the same boy.

At nine o'clock Lateesha announced that it was time for bed.

Nathan looked at her and smiled.

"No!" he said. The firmness in his voice told Lateesha that it was going to bee a long night.

Proofreading

4.24 Summer Challenge

It was tennis day at summer camp. Darci was to play Lora in the championship Match.

Darci looked at Lora and frowned. She doubted that she could beat Lora.

"Loras a great player," Darci said to Melissa her best friend.

"She is," said Melissa, "But she loses her cool. She tries to hit the ball as hard as she can every time. She hits a lot of balls out of bounds. Then she gets mad and hits them even harder. That makes her miss more."

"But how does that help me," said Darci. "I'll be lucky to return half of her shots."

"You have to play a steady game, said Melissa. "Don't make mistakes. Thats how your going to beat her."

"You mean she'll beat herself," said Darci.

Melissa nodded.

Not long after the match began Darci new her friend was right. When the match was finished Darci was the tennis champ.

4.25 Travelers

Captain Danos watched the main viewing screen on the bridge of his Spaceship. The tiny world grew on the screen. As it became larger oceans and land masses appeared threw patchy white clouds.

"It looks much like home" said Danos to Lieutenant Tarka.

"Yes it does." Tarka said.

"Does the planet have intelligent life," Danos asked?

Tarka checked some instruments.

"I think it does." he said. "I'm picking up radio transmissions."

"Are the inhabitants advanced enough for us to make contact," said Danos.

"Doubtful," Tarka said. "They seem primitive and warlike."

"Too bad," said Danos. "Whats the name of they're planet."

"Earth," said Tarka.

Captain Danos gave the order to pass bye Earth.

Proofreading

Answer Key

Part 1

Answers for the worksheets throughout this section will vary. Accept reasonable answers, stories, and articles.

Part 2

2.1 Sentences will vary. Accept reasonable sentences.

2.2 Answers may vary. Possible answers follow. 1. The dog barked through the night. 2. Tom slipped on the icy sidewalk. 3. Brianna almost cried when she stubbed her toe. 4. The little girl waited for her grandparents to come. 5. The thunder rumbled during the storm. 6. Paulo smiled at the thought of no homework. 7. Lila practiced the flute each night. 8. The river flooded because of the heavy rain.

2.3 Answers may vary. Possible answers follow. 1. Carl came home from school and did his homework. 2. It snowed all night, and school was canceled. 3. Susan likes to dance, but Staci, her sister, likes to sing. 4. The clouds grew darker, and the wind began to gust. 5. Amanda enjoys basketball, but she enjoys softball too. 6. It might rain tonight, or it might snow. 7. Tom could do his math homework, or he could work on his science project. 8. The puppy growled at the toy, but it was a playful growl.

2.4 Answers may vary. Possible answers follow. 2. After Luis finished his homework, he watched TV. 3. Because it rained all night, the river was rising. 4. When the computer crashed, Rashad was almost done with his science project. 5. Even though Carla had a terrible cold, she still went to dance practice. 6. Once the rain ended, the sky quickly cleared. 7. While it was raining, Trish finished reading *Char-*

lotte's Web. 8. During the worst part of the storm, lightning flashed and thunder exploded.

2.5 └Do you know the difference between *meteoroid*, *meteor*, and *meteorite*? Many people find these words confusing. └Meteoroids are chunks of rock or metal that speed through space. Some are very large and may be hundreds of feet wide. Others may be the size of a small stone. Most meteoroids orbit the sun. └Sometimes a meteoroid will enter the Earth's atmosphere. Friction with the atmosphere will cause it to heat up and burn. When a meteoroid begins to burn in the atmosphere, it leaves a streak of light. This is called a meteor, or shooting star. Most meteors burn up before they hit the ground. If a meteor does not burn completely, it will hit the Earth. A meteor that hits the Earth is called a meteorite. └If a meteor is big, this will cause a great explosion and much destruction. └Most meteoroids stay safely away from the Earth. Of those that enter the atmosphere, most burn up long before reaching the ground.

2.6 Answers may vary. Possible answers follow. 1. Dan likes to read. 2. Jenna is an excellent athlete. 3. Bradley had a lot of homework. 4. Christy couldn't find her keys. 5. Accept reasonable clues.

2.7 Answers may vary. Possible answers follow. 1. She needed to clean the house, set up decorations, set the table, and get the cake. 2. The wind picked up. Thunder could be heard in the distance. The first drops of rain began to fall. 3. He helped in the yard. He painted the fence. He washed the car. 4. The temperature was in the nineties. Everyone was hot. The land baked in the heat.

2.8 Answers may vary. Possible answers follow. 2. The storm ripped the big oak tree from the ground. 3. The puppy chased the ball. 4. Kevin dashed across the finish line ahead of the other fifth graders. 5. The winds of the storm shook the house. 6. Jess jumped at the strange noises. 7. Miguel blasted the ball over the fence. 8. It was impossible to see through the heavy, falling snow.

2.9 Answers may vary. Possible answers follow. 1. blazing 2. old; chilling 3. huge 4. great; stately 5. Red; beautiful 6. playful; spongy 7. exciting 8. tall; blue 9. icy 10. lonely; empty

2.10 Answers may vary. Possible answers follow. 1. completely 2. Soon 3. recently 4. softly 5. hard 6. often 7. usually 8. quickly 9. easily 10. carelessly

2.11 Answers may vary. Accept reasonable answers.

2.12 1. Jill was nervous. She could not stop fussing. This was her first piano recital, and she was afraid she would make mistakes. When her mother tried to assure her that she would do fine, Jill smiled. But she still felt nervous. When her piano instructor called her name, Jill stood. She took a deep breath and walked toward the piano at the front of the room. 2. Alvaro woke up early on Saturday. He knew it was going to be a busy day. That morning, he helped his father clean the garage. In the afternoon Alvaro went to soccer practice. He came back from practice around four P.M. He watched his little brother until dinner because his parents went shopping. After dinner Alvaro went online to find information for his science report. By the time Alvaro went to sleep that night, he was very tired.

2.13 2. The wind whipped the kite about. 3. Eduardo washed the dishes. 4. Gina gave the speech. 5. Clare designed the cover for the class magazine. 6. Carlos sang a solo in the fifth-grade concert. 7. The cat sneaked up on the bird. 8. The storm caused dangerous driving conditions.

2.14 Answers may vary. Possible answers follow. 2. The little girl whispered during the movie. 3. Tommy screamed when his toy broke. 4. The eagle soared over the valley. 5. Jason dodged the ball. 6. Melissa tiptoed across the room.

2.15 1. past 2. present 3. present 4. future 5. past 6. future

2.16 1. likes 2. play 3. enjoy 4. practices 5. lives 6. look 7. helps 8. come 9. fill 10. studies

2.17 I sighed, thinking of all the homework I had. I did not know where to begin.
   I looked at the pile of books on my desk. I knew I had better start if I wanted to meet my friends later.
   I opened my math book first. After I finished ten division problems, I did my spelling. Next I did my history.
   Finished at last, I went to see my friends. They were waiting for me at the basketball court.
   As soon as I got there, we chose teams and started a game.

2.18 Stories may vary, depending on the name of the point-of-view character. Accept reasonable stories.
   Too excited to sleep, Deanna woke up early. This was the day her father and she were going on a ten-kilometer bike tour. The goal of the tour was to raise money for charity. Deanna thought it would be a great day.
   By the time the tour began, she wasn't so sure. The sky had grown dark and a cool wind was blowing. She was worried that it would rain.
   All the time they rode, Deanna kept looking at the sky. Just as they came to the finish line, the first drops started to fall on them.
   Deanna smiled. It had been a great day after all.

2.19 Compare: Both elephants have trunks and eat grass and leaves. Contrast: African elephants are found mostly in Africa. The African elephant is larger and has bigger ears. Indian elephants are found mostly in India and Southeast Asia. Indian elephants are taller at the arch of the back.

2.20 Answers may vary. Possible answers follow. 1. plane, S 2. rabbit, S 3. monster, M 4. fox, S 5. torpedo, M 6. scream, M

Part 3
Revised articles and stories will vary. Possible revisions are provided.

3.1 The moon is the Earth's natural satellite. About 240,000 miles away, it is our closest neighbor in space. It is the only body in the solar system people have visited.

The moon is a barren, lifeless, and dangerous world. It has no atmosphere and no liquid water. The surface is covered with dust and craters. In the shade, the temperature on the moon can be as cold as −280° Fahrenheit. In sunlight, the temperature can be as hot as 260° Fahrenheit.

Scientists continue to study the moon. They hope that by learning more about the moon they will learn more about our solar system.

3.2 A geyser is a natural hot spring that shoots water and steam high into the air. Most geysers are found in the western United States, Iceland, and New Zealand.

Geysers occur when hot volcanic rock heats underground water to high temperatures. As the water is heated, it begins to boil. Steam forms and forces the water upward through cracks in the rock. Sometimes there is enough pressure to shoot the hot water and steam into the air.

The most famous geyser in the world is Old Faithful in Yellowstone National Park. Old Faithful erupts on average once every ninety-four minutes each day. Between 3,700 and 8,400 gallons of hot water shoot up to 170 feet in the air.

Watching a geyser is exciting. Geysers are one of nature's thrilling shows.

3.3 Modern roller coasters have their beginnings with Russian ice slides. The slides were first built in the mid-1600s.

The ice slides were big, wooden structures. Some were between seventy and eighty feet high. They were covered with thick ice. Large sleds sped down the slide along an icy path for hundreds of feet. The builders even constructed stairs for riders to walk up the slides.

Some historians believe the Russians also built the first true roller coaster in the late 1700s in St. Petersburg. It was a carriage with wheels.

From these simple beginnings, we have the super roller coasters of today. A person can only imagine what future coasters will be like.

3.4 Having healthy teeth is important. Strong, healthy teeth help you to chew your food properly. They help you to speak clearly and look your best.

To keep your teeth healthy, you must keep them clean. Brush your teeth at least twice each day, after breakfast and before bed. Brush for at least three minutes. Be sure to brush in the back and along the sides of your teeth. You should also clean your teeth with dental floss. The floss will clean places your toothbrush cannot reach. Finally, visit your dentist twice each year. The dentist will check for cavities and clean your teeth.

Strong, clean teeth will help to keep you healthy. Your teeth are something to smile about.

3.5 Exercising each day will help to keep you in good health. It will also help you think better, sleep better, and feel better.

Exercise helps your body stay fit. It causes you to breathe more deeply and makes your heart pump more strongly. It makes your muscles work harder and makes your body use more calories. Exercise helps to keep your body at a healthy weight.

You can exercise in many ways. You can walk, run, or jog. You can play sports. You can ride your bike. You can skate, swim, or dance. Any activity that makes your heart beat faster is good.

Exercise is important for your health. You should try to exercise every day.

3.6 The wandering albatross is a large seabird. When it spreads it wings, the wings measure up to twelve feet from tip to tip. This is the largest wingspread of any living bird.

Wandering albatrosses do not have a permanent home. They spend most of their lives flying over the oceans of the Southern Hemisphere, where they feed on small fish. They can sleep on the sea's surface when they become tired of flying. Like most seabirds, they drink seawater. They land on empty islands only to mate and make their nests.

Because of its size, the wandering albatross has few predators. The wandering albatross is thought to be one of the few birds to die of old age.

3.7 Pompeii was a city in ancient Italy. It was built a few miles south of Mt. Vesuvius, an active volcano. Pompeii was a wealthy city and was always busy with trade.

The day of August 24 in the year A.D. 79 began like any other. People awoke that day and began their chores. In the distance the volcano sent lazy dark smoke into the sky. But this was normal. No one was worried.

Without warning, the top of Vesuvius exploded. Great clouds of smoke and ash rose high into the sky. Soon the light of the sun was blocked and the sky became dark.

The eruption continued throughout the day and night. The city was covered with ash and molten rock. It is estimated that two thousand people died. The doomed city of Pompeii disappeared in a day.

3.8 The Oregon Trail was the most important pioneer route to the American Northwest. The trail was about two thousand miles long. It started in Independence, Missouri, and ended at the Columbia River in Oregon.

The journey over the trail was long, hard, and dangerous. The trip could take as long as six months. The pioneers faced many hardships. Terrible storms, illness, lack of food, and attacks by Native Americans were constant threats. Sometimes as many as half of the people of a wagon train died on the trail.

Despite the hardships, thousands of pioneers followed the trail. They believed that the Oregon Trail was a way to a new life.

3.9 Laura Ingalls was born in Pepin, Wisconsin, on February 7, 1867. She was the second daughter of Charles and Caroline Ingalls.

During her childhood, Laura traveled westward with her family in a covered wagon. The Ingalls family crossed Wisconsin, Kansas, and Minnesota. They finally settled in the Dakota Territory.

Laura loved living on the prairie. Life could be hard, but it was full of joy too. Laura enjoyed helping her parents with the chores.

When Laura grew up, she married Almanzo Wilder. Laura and Almanzo moved to Mansfield, Missouri, and built a home.

Laura remembered her family's pioneer days fondly. She would tell Rose, her daughter, stories about living on the prairie. Rose suggested that her mother write the stories down so that others could read them. These stories became the Little House series.

3.10 Rachel stood in her new room. Boxes were everywhere. The room was bigger than the room in her old house. But it did not feel like home.

Rachel missed her old house. She missed her old friends and was worried about making new friends.

After unpacking some boxes, Rachel went outside. She sat on the front steps. She looked around the pretty yard that was filled with colorful flowers and trees.

She noticed a girl from the house across the street walking toward her. The girl was about her own age.

"Hi, I'm Danielle," the girl said. "But my friends call me Dani. . . ."

3.11 Jason stood in his messy room. He was upset.

He could not find his science report. He had finished it yesterday right after school. Then he had gone out to play with his friends.

He looked at his messy desk. First he searched through the books and papers on it. Next he searched the messy drawers in the desk. Then he searched his messy dresser. Finally, he searched under his messy bed.

He tried to remember where he put the report. Suddenly, he remembered.

He picked up his knapsack. The report was in a folder. He had put it in the knapsack yesterday so that he would not lose it.

Jason heard the school bus. He grabbed his knapsack and hurried to the door.

3.12 Maria stood in front of the big roller coaster. Carlos, her younger brother, was with her.

The roller coaster was called the Monster. Maria had been looking forward to riding it for weeks, but now she was not sure.

The Monster was high and fast, and had three loops. Maria liked fast rides, but this one scared her.

"Come on, Maria," said Carlos. "Let's get in line." He took her hand and started pulling her.

At first Maria did not move. It was as if her feet would not go.

"Maria, come on," said Carlos. "You're not afraid, are you?"

Maria smiled weakly. If her little brother was not afraid, she should not be afraid either.

"Let's go," Maria said. She led Carlos to the line.

3.13 One second was left in the championship game between the Hawks and Cougars. The score was 38 to 38.

Kevin Williams, the Cougars' youngest player, was at the foul line. If he made either of his two foul shots, the Cougars would be champions. But Kevin was not a good foul shooter.

The referee gave him the ball.

He took a deep breath and bounced the ball to calm himself.

He looked up at the basket, aimed, and let the ball go. It bounced off the rim. The home crowd groaned.

The referee handed Kevin the ball again. Once more he bounced the ball to steady himself. He aimed and let it go.

He watched the ball fall perfectly through the net.

3.14 The sun is a star. Like other stars, it is a giant ball of burning gases. It is made up mostly of hydrogen.

Inside the sun, hydrogen atoms are fused (forced together) to make helium. Great amounts of energy are produced. Some of this energy reaches the Earth as light and heat. The temperature on the surface of the sun is about 11,000° Fahrenheit. Inside the sun, near the center, the temperature is about 35 million degrees Fahrenheit.

The sun makes life possible on the Earth. Without the sun, the Earth would be a cold, dark, lifeless planet.

3.15 Bears are large mammals. There are several kinds of bears.

Black bears were once found throughout North America, but now they are found mostly in wilderness areas. Black bears are one of the smallest bears. They weigh between two hundred and four hundred pounds.

Grizzly bears are among the most dangerous bears and can weigh up to one thousand pounds. Grizzlies hunt other animals for food. Grizzlies may be brown, black, or cream-colored. The fur on their shoulders and backs is often tipped with white. This gives them a "grizzled" look.

Polar bears are found on the islands of the Arctic Ocean. They may be ten feet tall and weigh up to fifteen hundred pounds. Polar bears hunt seals, young walruses, and fish. Their thick white coats keep them warm in icy temperatures.

Bears are found in many parts of the world. They are among nature's most interesting animals.

3.16 Many people have heard of Smokey Bear. They know Smokey is a symbol for fire prevention, but not everyone knows the story of the real Smokey.

On a spring day in 1950, a terrible fire burned parts of New Mexico. Firefighters found a baby black bear in a tree. The cub had climbed the tree to try to escape the flames. But his paws and back were burned. The men gently took the cub from the tree. They did not know what to do with him. A rancher who had been helping the firefighters offered to take the injured cub home.

A forest ranger heard about the cub. He drove to the ranch and had the injured cub flown to Santa Fe. A veterinarian there treated his injuries.

Eventually the cub was sent to Washington, D.C., and was given a home in the National Zoo. The cub became known as Smokey Bear.

3.17 Johnny Appleseed was a real man. His name was John Chapman. He was born in 1774 in Leominster, Massachusetts.

When settlers moved westward, John went with them. For nearly fifty years John planted apple trees in what became the states of Ohio, Michigan, Illinois, and Indiana. People called John the Apple Tree Man or Johnny Appleseed.

John worked alone. As he walked across the wilderness, he would find a good spot for planting. He would clear the land and plant apple seeds. He would build a brush fence around the spot to keep animals out. In time, an orchard would fill the spot.

John Chapman died in 1845. The apple orchards he left behind were a gift to the settlers who came after him.

3.18 With nervous fingers Tamara tightened the laces of her ice skates. She took a deep breath.

"Don't worry," her coach said. "You'll do fine."

That made Tamara worry even more. That was what people told her last winter. Tamara remembered trying to jump and turn in the air for the first time. She would never forget the terrible pain of her ankle breaking. Her ankle hurt badly for days, and her slow recovery took months.

Tamara started skating again a few weeks ago. She had not tried to jump and spin, but she would today.

Tamara stood and stepped onto the ice. Her heart was thumping.

"Good luck," said her coach.

Tamara nodded.

She skated around the rink and tried to build up her courage.
She began to skate faster and faster. She lifted off the ice, rose, and spun.
She landed perfectly!

3.19 When ancient sailors reported seeing sea monsters, they might have seen a giant squid. The giant squid is a frightening animal.

The name *giant squid* fits this creature. The giant squid can grow to be 150 feet long. Its big eyes can be 3 feet across. It has long tentacles that it uses to catch prey.

The giant squid is one of the fastest creatures in the ocean. It can draw water into its body and force the water out. That shoots the animal forward like a rocket.

Giant squid live deep in the ocean, but sometimes they come to the surface. If ancient sailors saw a giant squid on the surface, they could have mistaken it for a sea monster.

3.20 John Montagu was a nobleman who lived in England in the 1700s. He was the fourth Earl of Sandwich and a well-known gambler.

When he was gambling, he would sit at the table for hours. One day he was gambling and got hungry. But he did not want to leave the game. He sent a servant to bring him meat between two slices of bread.

Other gamblers thought this was a good idea. When they got hungry, they said something like, "I'll have what Sandwich had." Soon the name Sandwich came to mean meat between two slices of bread.

The sandwich was named after the Earl of Sandwich in 1762. Since then, countless sandwiches have been made.

3.21 When most people think of dinosaurs, they think of big creatures. But there were little dinosaurs too.

The smallest dinosaur is thought to be a microraptor. This dinosaur was about sixteen inches long and was about the size of a crow.

Saltopus was a little bigger than a microraptor. It was about two feet long, the size of a small cat. It walked on two legs, had a long head, and had dozens of sharp teeth.

Compsognathus was about the size of a big chicken. It was about three feet long. It had two thin legs, three-toed feet, and a long tail. It had a pointed head and sharp teeth.

Scientists may discover even smaller dinosaurs someday. But most people will probably continue to think of dinosaurs as big creatures.

3.22 Wiley Post was born in Grand Plain, Texas, in 1899. Although he did not have much formal schooling, he became one of the most famous early pilots.

In 1931, Post and his navigator, Harold Charles Gatty, flew around the world. They made the flight in eight days, fifteen hours, and fifty-one minutes. They set a new world record.

In 1933, Post decided to fly around the world by himself. He set a new record of seven days, eighteen hours, and forty-nine minutes.

Wiley Post died on August 15, 1935. His plane crashed at Point Barrow, Alaska. He was called a national hero.

3.23 Kareem woke up early on Saturday. He had a busy day planned.

After breakfast, Kareem went to soccer practice. He liked soccer and was the goalie for his team.

After lunch, Kareem helped his father in the yard. They raked leaves and trimmed the hedges. As his father mowed the lawn, Kareem weeded the flower beds. They worked in the yard all afternoon.

In the evening, Kareem's friends, David and Charles, came. The boys decided to watch a movie. After his friends went home, Kareem watched TV a little while with his parents.

Tired, he soon went to bed. It had been a busy day.

3.24 The platypus is a strange, unusual animal. It is a mammal, but it also has traits of a duck. Another name for the platypus is the duckbill.

Platypuses are found in Australia. They live in burrows along the banks of rivers.

An adult platypus is about fourteen inches in length. It has a long body and a flat tail. It uses its tail for swimming.

The platypus has many traits of mammals. It is warm-blooded, has fur, and feeds its young milk.

But the platypus also has some traits of ducks. Instead of a nose and mouth, the platypus has a leathery bill. It has webbed feet for swimming, and it lays eggs. A baby platypus hatches from an egg.

The platypus is truly a strange, unusual animal.

3.25 Daedalus and his son Icarus were imprisoned on the island of Crete. In hopes of escaping, Daedalus thought of a dangerous and daring plan. He would build wings of wax and feathers for Icarus and himself.

Daedalus began his work. When the day came that the wings were done, he called to Icarus. He warned Icarus not to fly too close to the sun. The heat would melt the wax and the wings would fall apart.

Icarus promised his father he would be careful. But once they set off, the boy was overcome with the thrill of flying like a bird.

Daedalus saw his son flying higher and higher. He called to him that he was too close to the sun. Yet the boy kept going higher.

Soon the wax on Icarus's wings began to melt. Feathers started to fall off. The boy flapped the wings wildly, but the wings came apart. Icarus fell into the sea and drowned.

Part 4

In a few articles and stories, corrections may vary depending on context. This is particularly true in the case of commas. In these cases, accept reasonable corrections. Corrected articles and stories follow.

4.1 The Gila monster is not a monster. It is a lizard. It is the largest lizard in the United States. It is also the only poisonous lizard in our country.

The Gila monster is found in the desert areas of Arizona, Nevada, Utah, and New Mexico. It is named after the Gila River.

An adult Gila monster is easy to recognize. It is about two feet long and weighs between three and five pounds. It has a thick body and short legs. Its black, scaly body is covered with orange, pink, and yellow spots.

The poison of a Gila monster is usually not strong enough to kill humans. But the bite of the lizard is painful.

4.2 Do you know how to study for tests? Here are some suggestions.

On the days leading up to the test, listen to any reviews your teacher gives. This will help you find out what may be on the test. You will be able to study the right material. If you have any questions about the material, ask your teacher.

Begin studying a day or two before the test. Go over your notes and key parts of your textbook. Do not wait until the last minute to study. Students who study ahead of time usually do better than those who cram.

On the day of the test be confident. People who study do better than people who do not study.

4.3 Katie woke up early on Saturday. She was too excited to sleep. Today was the day of her family's picnic.

Each year the Morgan family met at Ellis Park for a picnic. All of Katie's aunts, uncles, and cousins would be there.

After breakfast Katie helped her mother pack food in coolers. They packed sandwiches, salads, and desserts.

The drive to the park seemed to take forever. As they entered the park, Katie's father headed for Lake Ellis, where the picnic grounds were located. Nearing the lake, Katie saw that people were already there.

She smiled. This would be a great day.

4.4 Frogs and toads are amphibians. They are animals that can live both in water and on land. Although frogs and toads are much alike, they are different too. Do you know how they are different?

Frogs spend much of their lives in water. Their bodies are usually slimmer than the bodies of toads, they have smooth skin, and they have long legs for jumping.

Toads spend most of their lives on land. Their bodies are usually thicker than the bodies of frogs, they have warty skin, and they have shorter back legs.

Of course, for most people these are not very big differences. To them, frogs and toads are more alike than different.

4.5 Throughout history many plants and animals have become extinct. These plants and animals are no longer alive anywhere on our planet. Plants and animals become extinct for many reasons.

Big changes in climate can cause plants and animals to become extinct. If the climate of an area that once got much rain becomes very dry, some plants and animals may die out.

Sometimes people change the land where plants and animals live. For example, people cut down forests. They may use wood to build houses, or they may clear land for farming. The plants and animals that lived there may die.

Overhunting can cause animals to become extinct. Before the settlers came, buffalo ranged across the American Great Plains. By the end of the nineteenth century buffaloes were hunted almost to extinction.

Every effort should be made to protect plants and animals from extinction. Once a plant or animal becomes extinct, it is too late.

4.6 Marissa went down the hall toward her classroom. She felt foolish coming back to school. But she had forgotten her history book. Without her history book, she wouldn't be able to study for the big history test tomorrow.

History was a hard subject for Marissa. If she wanted a high grade on her report card, she had to study.

Just before she got to the classroom, she saw a paper on the floor. When she picked the paper up, her eyes widened. It was the test's answer key.

This was her chance to get a good grade. She held the key for a long moment.

That would be cheating, and Marissa wasn't a cheater.

She went into her classroom. Her teacher, Ms. Carter, was there. Marissa went to the desk and handed the key to Ms. Carter.

4.7 With its oceans, lakes, and rivers, the Earth has plenty of water. But not all parts of the Earth have a lot of water. About one-fifth of the Earth's land is desert.

Deserts are dry areas of land. Some deserts get only an inch or two of rainfall every year.

Although it is hard for life to survive in deserts, many plants and animals make the desert their home. Plants such as the cactus live in deserts. Animals such as snakes, lizards, and camels live in deserts too.

People also live in or near deserts. Many of these people believe that deserts have a special beauty. This beauty is found nowhere else on our planet.

4.8 Earthquakes are more common than most people think. Thousands of earthquakes occur each year, but most are so weak they aren't felt. Only about one out of five hundred earthquakes causes damage.

In the past, people didn't know what caused earthquakes. Today scientists know that the Earth's crust, its outer layer, is divided into great pieces. These pieces, called *plates*, are made of rock. The plates move slowly in different directions. They may move past each other, away from each other, or toward each other. Sometimes a long crack, called a fault, forms between plates. If enough stress builds up along a fault, an earthquake occurs.

Minor earthquakes cause little damage. Major quakes can destroy buildings, bridges, and roads. They can cause thousands of deaths.

4.9 It was field day at Manuel's school. As he waited for his turn to run, Manuel was worried. He was the fastest boy in the fifth grade, but that could change today.

Mr. Wilkins, Manuel's teacher, called the last four boys to the starting line.

Manuel stepped forward. This was a race against time. Whoever ran the fastest would be the fastest runner in the fifth grade.

Manuel took a deep breath and bent his legs. Every muscle was ready. He looked at the finish line at the end of the field. Another teacher, Ms. Edwards, was there with a stopwatch.

"On your mark!" said Mr. Wilkins. "Get set! Go!"

The boys began. Manuel took powerful strides. He heard the other kids cheering, but his thoughts were only on running. He was pulling ahead.

Manuel crossed the line first.

"Sixteen point three seconds!" Ms. Edwards said.

Manuel smiled. That was the best time of the day. He was still the fastest runner in the fifth grade.

4.10
123 Mountain Road
High Point, WA 00000
September 25, 2006

Mr. William Connors, Circulation Manager
Rugged Outdoors Magazine
50 Carter Street
Centerville, CA 00000

Dear Mr. Connors:

I would like to subscribe to *Rugged Outdoors Magazine*. Enclosed is a check for $19.95 for a subscription for one year.

Thank you.

Yours truly,
Jon Petersen

4.11 Jimmy and I are best friends. We've been best friends since kindergarten.

Some kids think it's strange that a girl and a boy in fifth grade are best friends. But Jimmy and I have a lot in common.

We live next door to each other. We both like sports, we like the same type of music, and we like the same kinds of movies. But most important, we just like hanging out together. Jimmy's easy to talk to, and he's always willing to help when I have a problem. I do the same for him.

No matter what happens, I know I can count on Jimmy. I suppose that's what's best about being best friends.

4.12 Arbor Day is a day for planting trees. All fifty states in the U.S. celebrate Arbor Day.

Julius Sterling Morton (1832–1902) founded the first Arbor Day in Nebraska on April 10, 1872. Morton believed that Nebraska's land could be improved by the planting of trees.

Nebraska's first Arbor Day was a great success. People planted more than one million trees. A second Arbor Day took place in 1884 and also was successful. In 1885, Nebraska made Arbor Day a holiday and set April 22nd to celebrate it. April 22nd was Julius Sterling Morton's birthday.

In the following years, other states set aside their own Arbor Days. Although the dates vary because of climate, Arbor Day remains a day for planting trees. It is a day people throughout the country can celebrate our environment.

4.13 Jason looked at the darkening sky. He turned to Martin, his friend.

"I bet it's going to rain," Jason said.

"It'll hold off until after the game," said Martin.

The two boys had just arrived at the baseball field. Some of the players of both teams were already there. This was the first game of the season, and all the boys were excited.

Coach Smith instructed the boys to begin warm-ups.

Jason and Martin took their places with their teammates and began stretching.

Jason looked back at the sky. He loved baseball and had been looking forward to this first game for weeks.

"You worry too much," said Martin. "From the looks of those clouds, it won't rain for a while."

"I hope you're right," said Jason.

A little while later the game was ready to start.

"Play ball!" the umpire called.

"See," said Martin. "You worry too much."

Jason smiled. "Maybe you're right."

4.14 Everybody in my family likes to read. Books, magazines, and newspapers are everywhere in our home.

My father reads the newspaper every morning. He reads the *New York Times* on the train to work. He also reads magazines. His favorite is *Newsweek*.

My mother likes to read novels. She reads a new novel every week. She likes mysteries the best.

Stephie, my sister, likes short stories and poems. One of her favorite short stories is "The Open Window" by H. H. Munro. Her favorite poem is Robert Frost's "The Road Not Taken."

I like to read novels. My favorites are science fiction. If I had to pick one favorite, I would choose *A Wrinkle in Time* by Madeleine L' Engle.

4.15 Kyra stood on the top of the mountain. She looked down the ski slope. Breakneck Trail disappeared in the distance. She took a deep breath to steady herself.

"Don't be afraid," said Mia, her big sister. "You can make it down."

"I'm not worried about making it down," said Kyra. She forced a smile. "I'm worried about how many pieces I'll be in."

Mia patted her on the shoulder. "You don't have to do this," she said.

"Yes, I do," said Kyra. "This is the only trail on this mountain I've never gone down."

Mia smiled. "Keep your knees bent," she said, "and remember to lean into the turns."

"Wish me luck," Kyra said. She pushed off with her poles and started down the trail.

As she picked up speed, she heard Mia's voice behind her.

"Good luck."

4.16 What causes sound? The sounds of a crying baby, the slamming of a door, or the roar of a jet's engines are all produced in the same way.

Sound is caused by vibrations. When something vibrates, it moves back and forth rapidly. Imagine pulling a string on a guitar. As the string vibrates, it makes a sound.

Vibrating objects cause the molecules in the air around them to move. As the molecules move, the vibrations travel through the air in waves. When these waves reach your ear, you hear the sound.

As sound waves move away from a vibrating object, they become weaker. A sound becomes fainter the farther away you are from its source.

4.17 Have you ever played checkers? If you have, you have played one of the world's oldest games.

Games similar to checkers were played by the ancient Egyptians about thirty-five hundred years ago. A form of the game was also played in ancient Greece. The modern form of checkers appeared about five hundred years ago.

Checkers is a game of skill. Two players play against each other. Each player has twelve playing pieces on a board that has sixty-four squares. The goal of the game is to capture an opponent's pieces. The best players think ahead and take advantage of their opponent's mistakes.

Checkers is played around the world. Minor rules vary somewhat from country to country, but the basic game is the same.

4.18 Most accidents happen at home. Although nobody can prevent every accident, you can prevent many accidents by being careful and using common sense.

Many accidents occur in the kitchen. Always be careful around a stove so that you don't get burned. Don't leave paper towels, napkins, or cloths near the stove. Handle knives with care. Don't touch their sharp blades, and always cut away from your body. Keep knives in a safe place where young children can't get them.

Many accidents also occur in the bathroom. Never use electrical appliances such as a hair dryer near water. Use a rubber mat to prevent anyone from slipping in the bathtub. Keeping soap in a soap dish will help prevent people from slipping on it.

Accidents can happen to anyone. But using common sense and being careful can reduce the chances of an accident happening to you.

4.19 Hallie took her seat in the boat. She was not pleased. Her parents and she were spending one of their vacation days looking for whales. Her mom called it whale-watching. Hallie would have liked to spend the day at the lake, where her parents had rented a cabin for the week.

"This will be exciting," Hallie's mother said.

"I'd rather be swimming at the lake," Hallie said.

"You can swim every day for the rest of the week," said her father. "But you can't see a whale every day."

Hallie didn't understand what could be so great about seeing a whale. She pulled up the hood of her sweatshirt to block the cool breeze.

It was early afternoon when one of the boat's crewmen pointed ahead.

"There!" he cried.

Hallie turned and saw a fantastic creature rise from the water.

"It's beautiful," she said, and she forgot all about swimming.

4.20 Colors make the world a brighter place. Imagine how dull the world would be without colors.

Colors can be divided into three kinds: primary, secondary, and intermediate.

The primary colors are red, yellow, and blue. These are known as the basic colors. They can't be made by mixing any other colors.

The secondary colors are orange, green, and violet. Secondary colors are made by mixing two primary colors. Mixing red and yellow makes orange. Mixing yellow and blue makes green. Mixing blue and red makes violet.

Intermediate colors are made by mixing primary and secondary colors. Mixing white or black with colors will make them lighter or darker.

It is remarkable that all colors are based on combinations of red, yellow, and blue. What a colorful world the Earth is!

4.21 I was doing my homework when Annie, my little sister, came running into my room.

"Cassie, come quick!" she cried.

"What's wrong?" I said.

"It's Sasha!" Annie said between sobs. "She's stuck in a big tree." Sasha was our cat.

I followed her downstairs and out the front door.

I looked up at the big oak tree in our yard. Sure enough, Sasha was sitting on a high branch. Although she had climbed up, she was afraid to climb down.

"Sasha, come down," I said. But all I received was a sad meow.

There wasn't anything I could do except to keep calling Sasha to come down. But the cat wouldn't budge.

Fortunately, my father and mother soon came home from work. My father got the ladder from the garage and got Sasha.

I smiled as Annie scolded the silly cat.

"Sasha, don't ever do that again," she said.

4.22 When sunlight strikes water droplets in the air, a rainbow may form. The rainbow makes an arc in the sky. Sometimes its ends seem to touch the Earth.

Why does a rainbow appear when sunlight hits water droplets? The answer lies in sunlight. A ray of sunlight contains all the colors of the spectrum: red, orange, yellow, green, blue, and violet. Tiny water droplets separate the sunlight into its different colors. Under the right conditions, that creates a rainbow.

Rainbows most often are seen near the end of a rain shower. But they can also be seen in the spray of a waterfall, a fountain, or a garden hose.

According to legend, a pot of gold is at the end of a rainbow. Of course, no one can ever reach the end of a rainbow. As you approach a rainbow, it seems to move farther away and soon disappears.

4.23 Lateesha rang the doorbell to the home of Mr. and Mrs. Morgan. This was the first time she was to babysit for their son Nathan. She hoped Nathan, who was only five years old, would behave. Her friend Christina had babysat for Nathan once, and she would never do it again.

Mrs. Morgan opened the door with a big smile.

Lateesha saw Nathan standing in the living room. He was smiling too. He seemed like a nice boy.

After Mrs. Morgan gave Lateesha instructions, she and her husband got ready to leave.

"Remember, Lateesha," Mrs. Morgan said at the door, "Nathan must be in bed by nine."

"I won't forget," Lateesha said.

For the next two hours she read to Nathan, they colored, and they watched TV. Nathan was so delightful that Lateesha began to wonder if Christina had babysat for the same boy.

At nine o'clock Lateesha announced that it was time for bed.

Nathan looked at her and smiled.

"No!" he said. The firmness in his voice told Lateesha that it was going to be a long night.

4.24 It was tennis day at summer camp. Darci was to play Lora in the championship match.

Darci looked at Lora and frowned. She doubted that she could beat Lora.

"Lora's a great player," Darci said to Melissa, her best friend.

"She is," said Melissa, "but she loses her cool. She tries to hit the ball as hard as she can every time. She hits a lot of balls out of bounds. Then she gets mad and hits them even harder. That makes her miss more."

"But how does that help me?" said Darci. "I'll be lucky to return half of her shots."

"You have to play a steady game," said Melissa. "Don't make mistakes. That's how you're going to beat her."

"You mean she'll beat herself," said Darci.

Melissa nodded.

Not long after the match began, Darci knew her friend was right. When the match was finished, Darci was the tennis champ.

4.25 Captain Danos watched the main viewing screen on the bridge of his spaceship. The tiny world grew on the screen. As it became larger, oceans and land masses appeared through patchy white clouds.

"It looks much like home," said Danos to Lieutenant Tarka.

"Yes, it does," Tarka said.

"Does the planet have intelligent life?" Danos asked.

Tarka checked some instruments.

"I think it does," he said. "I'm picking up radio transmissions."

"Are the inhabitants advanced enough for us to make contact?" said Danos.

"Doubtful," Tarka said. "They seem primitive and warlike."

"Too bad," said Danos. "What's the name of the planet?"

"Earth," said Tarka.

Captain Danos gave the order to pass by Earth.

Index